Sacred Objects, Sacred Space

Everyday Tools for the Modern-Day Witch

Dayna Winters
Patricia Gardner
Angela Kaufman

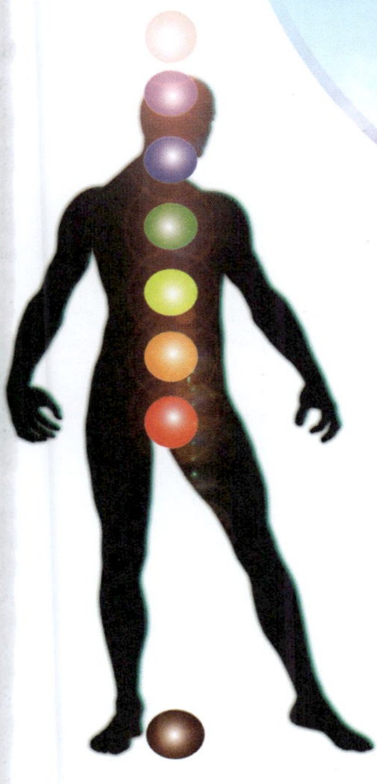

Schiffer Publishing Ltd®
4880 Lower Valley Road • Atglen, PA 19310

Dedication

We dedicate this book to
Elaine, Raymond, and Constance Austro.
Thank you for sharing your sacred space with us and with others who choose to take the Magickal journey.

Image Courtesies:
page 22: *Illustration by Angela Kaufman; graphic designed by Dayna Winters.*
page 102: *Graphic by Dayna Winters, using elements from Graphic Allusions.*
page 114: *Courtesy of Elaine, Raymond, and Constance Austro.*
page 115: *Courtesy of Elaine, Raymond, and Constance Austro.*
page 120: *Graphic designed by Dayna Winters using elements from Graphic Allusions.*
page 144: *Illustration by Angela Kaufman; graphic by Dayna Winters.*
page 164: *Graphic made by Dayna Winters using elements from Graphic Allusions.*
page 185: *Graphic designed by Dayna Winters using elements from Anita-Lee Creations and Graphic Allusions.*

All text and photos by authors
Ouija is a registered trademark of Hasbro, Inc.

Other Schiffer Books By The Author:

Wicca: What's the Real Deal?: Breaking Through the Misconceptions
ISBN 978-0-7643-3908-0 $17.99

Library of Congress Control Number: 2013930053

Designed by Mark David Bowyer
Type set in Brush Script MT / Book Antiqua

ISBN: 978-0-7643-4291-2
Printed in China

Published by Schiffer Publishing, Ltd.
4880 Lower Valley Road
Atglen, PA 19310
Phone: (610) 593-1777; Fax: (610) 593-2002
E-mail: Info@schifferbooks.com

In Europe, Schiffer books are distributed by
Bushwood Books
6 Marksbury Ave.
Kew Gardens
Surrey TW9 4JF England
Phone: 44 (0) 20 8392 8585;
Fax: 44 (0) 20 8392 9876
E-mail: info@bushwoodbooks.co.uk
Website: www.bushwoodbooks.co.uk

Contents

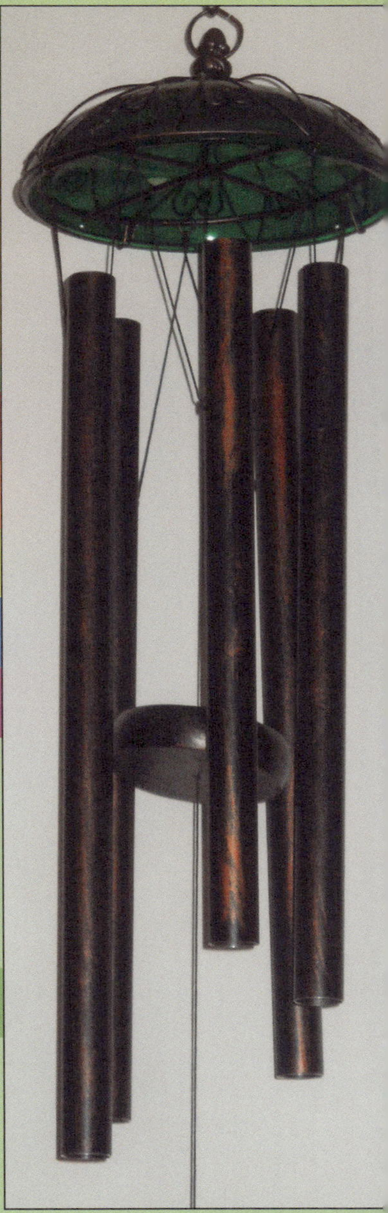

Acknowledgments

As with the creation of any book, it is necessary to thank a number of people. We first want to thank our families for their tremendous support during the research and writing process. We also want to express our gratitude to Schiffer Publishing for allowing us to put together this body of work, and we want to thank Dinah Roseberry, our editor, for always being available whenever we need assistance. In addition, we are thankful for the marketing team at Schiffer for the amazing work that they do. Special thanks go to Tracey and Lyn, for reviewing our work and for providing us with feedback. We are also grateful for the assistance of John L. Turner MD for his insightful advice, assistance, and for writing the foreword for this book. Finally, we remain forever grateful to the God and Goddess and the many blessings in our lives.

Foreword

John L. Turner, MD

My introduction to the authors occurred after an appearance on their radio show to discuss my new book, *Medicine, Miracles, and Manifestations: A Doctor's Journey Through the Worlds of Divine Intervention, Near-Death Experiences, and Universal Energy.* I came to know these ladies as voices on the phone and in the ether of the Internet. However, I knew little, if any, about their work as Wiccan practitioners and elders in the pagan community. They kindly gave all the time to discuss my work and they had no time to mention theirs. When I was asked to review their new book, *Sacred Objects, Sacred Space,* I gladly agreed, little knowing that after reading about their practices, my early attempts at manifestation could have been greatly enhanced had I known about the tools and *modus operandi* of the Wiccan practitioner.

By way of explanation, I will relate a quick story of what happened many years ago when I first understood multiple simultaneous dimensions, the spiritual world, and omnipresent and extraordinarily omnipotent universal energy. I had accumulated a great deal of knowledge, but, as mentioned in Dan Millman's *The Peaceful Warrior,* knowledge is not the same as wisdom. We become wise when we can put our knowledge to work for us and we must apply the proper leverage to universal energy. This requires careful focusing of our intent.

To wit, the thought occurred those many years ago, that a spread of pasture land with a valley and waterfall would be an idyllic spot for me to occasionally rusticate during the rare off-time as a busy neurosurgeon, the only such specialist on the Big Island of Hawaii. Such a spot was, so to speak, just what the doctor ordered. I knew it would be possible to bring this material substance into my reality. A big request? Not really, because even at this early stage, it was clear to me that all things are possible, and it is a matter of tweaking things for the better.

My *tools* were fashioned with the care and intent that the authors describe in this book. I removed the folding doors from a large 8 x 7 x 3 foot closet and with the assistance of my aged but energetic mother, we placed mirrors at both ends inside the space, installed indirect lighting at the top and put a beautiful large mural on the back wall: a picture of a forest stream that I knew just had to end in a waterfall as the flowing water returned to the ocean.

I installed sliding glass doors, tinted a light bronze, and as the *coup de manifestation*, a set of vertical mirrored blinds that could be remotely open and closed, and rotated to create a variety of reflections, just as if this stream would shimmer into and out of existence, as sounds of gentle water and birds issued forth from the closet.

Two years passed. Then, quite suddenly, I found myself driving up a dirt road, not far from the center of town. A tall man ran to the gate, holding a shotgun and accompanied by two large dogs. I explained that somehow, from a stranger whose name I didn't remember, I heard that his property was for sale. As part of this manifestation, his demeanor, of course, changed to a smile and a wide grin as he informed me that I had come to the right place. Indeed I had! A lovely two bedroom cottage with a 180-degree ocean view and the remainder of the scenario, from a back *lanai* (porch), looked down into a fertile valley which at one end revealed a beautiful 50-foot flowing waterfall. And above this waterfall? The stream, exactly as the one in the mural that I had applied to the back closet wall! Yes, I had materialized all of this on a 21-acre parcel in the beauty and holiness of Hawaii.

However, it took two or three years to do this, just under 1/30th of a lifetime. In retrospect, I now understand that the mural, the speakers, the dimmable-lighting, the sliding doors, and mirrored blinds were like Wiccan tools that I had carefully crafted and, in a way, cleansed with my focused intent of bringing such property into existence.

My point in telling this story is that had I known about the *tools* (amulets, bells, censers, bolines athames, etc.) and the practices described in this book and in their prior, and highly-recommended book *Wicca: What's the Real Deal?*, I could have used tried and true Wiccan techniques and practices to energize my focused will, personal energy, and intent, which would have allowed the waterfall manifestation to appear much sooner than it did. I now understand that there are no coincidences and that in this universe, everything is perfect and just as it should be, and that there are ways to adjust this perfection to make it even better.

This book is indispensable to the Wiccan. It covers it all. I give kudos to the authors on their concise descriptions of the essential tools of the trade. Through their work, the reader will learn how to properly utilize many tools as you continue your Magickal journey through the physical reality that we know as *life*. If you already have it down, this book is a very handy reference volume for the *crafty Witch.*

—John L. Turner, MD
Medicine, Miracles, and Manifestations: A Doctor's Journey Through the Worlds of Divine Intervention, Near-Death Experiences, and Universal Energy

Introduction

Mother, Maiden, and Crone,
Hear the words I intone,
Father, Sage, and Son,
This circle casting has begun.
Ancestors, Guardians, and Elements four,
Your presence here I implore.
Protect us now in this place,
Now transformed into sacred space.

If you are a neophyte just learning about Magickal applications and the use of ritual tools, *Sacred Objects, Sacred Space* is a book that explains the myriad uses of such tools, and the symbolism associated with Magickal paraphernalia. The book will also offer you advice on the care, maintenance, and cautions you should implement when dealing with your tools on a physical and spiritual level. We supply neophytes with advice on how to make mundane items Magickal, and there are tips for how to make or substitute tools with similar items that will work with equal effectiveness.

Sacred Objects, Sacred Space is a body of work that is ideal for the adept practitioner as well. First, the work will deepen the practitioner's understanding of tools and their symbolic significance: This can later lead to more meaningful and intensified Magickal workings. Additionally, many adept students of Magick, after learning of the basic tools and their uses, forget to take the extra step of integrating Magick into their everyday existence. *Sacred Objects, Sacred Space* has been written so that you can put the advice shared herein to practical use, and so that you can begin to live a truly Magickal life. The authors hope that you, the reader, can learn from this book how to weave Magick into your everyday experiences so that your life becomes even more spiritually fulfilling. We also hope that non-practitioners will use this book, especially readers who seek to understand the practices of a practitioner of the Magickal arts.

How to Use This Book

If you are a neophyte just learning the art of Witchcraft, we suggest that you read this book from beginning to end so that you can learn about all of the potential tools available to you, and the ins and outs of establishing sacred space. We have broken down the book into five chapters, the first four focusing on tools of the craft:

Chapter 1 focuses on altar tools.
Chapter 2 examines additional essentials.
Chapter 3 reveals an array of meditation tools available to the practitioner.
Chapter 4 focuses on tools used in divination.
Chapter 5 explores how to establish sacred space, as well as how to weave Magickal energies throughout the home or other spaces by using simple techniques.

If you are an adept, you have the option of reading the book from beginning to end, but you can also use *Sacred Objects, Sacred Space* as a reference book by simply using the information you need. For instance, if you are looking for creative tips on how to decorate, make, or substitute certain tools, you can find such information in our "For the Crafty Witch" section; or if you want some cautionary advice on tools, you can view the care, maintenance, and caution sections as a reference. Please note that the "Crafty Witch" sections supplied with each tool offer suggested crafts as well as clever or cunning ways for making substitutions for tools described. There really is no wrong way to use this book, and you will find that *Sacred Objects, Sacred Space* is a reference you can use repeatedly in the future.

Key Terminology in Tool and Sacred Space Preparation

You need to know some terms as you examine the different tools available to you, and their preparation for use in Magick. Understanding the differences between the terms offered here will help you fully understand the measures you are taking as you ready each tool for use. When getting your tools prepared for use or caring for them in the future, it is important to know the difference between a cleansing, blessing, consecration, charging, and an anointing. You also need to know the meaning of certain movements or actions you are required to make while preparing your tools for use.

Deosil / Widdershins Movements

When performing rituals or spells, you will sometimes note instructions involving deosil or widdershins movements. *Deosil* comes from the Celtic *deasil;* the latter word is combination of *deas*, meaning on the right side or right hand, and *Syl*, the Celtic term for sun.[1] Deosil (pronounced *dee-oh-sil, day-oh-sil, jessel, or dah-sul*) is movement in a clockwise direction or movement from an eastern to western direction;[2] you can use this motion to create positive energies or to draw energies to you. The term Widdershins (pronounced *Widder-shins*) comes from the Celtic *Widdersinnis* or *Withershins*, meaning movement from "left to right or from west to east."[3] Widdershins is movement in a counter clockwise direction; thus, it serves to repel negative energies.

Receptive / Projective Hand

When performing spells or rituals, you will sometimes note instructions pertaining to the use of your receptive or projective hand. Your receptive hand is your non-dominant hand. Your projective hand is your dominant hand or the hand you use the most for writing. If you are ambidextrous, you can use either hand as your projective or receptive hand.

Cleansing / Clearing

When you cleanse a person, place, or thing, you are purging the object of negative associations and energies. Cleansing is a transformative act; one that allows you to banish or eject negative forces from a chosen object so that you can use an untainted tool or object in Magickal applications. Cleansing differs from a blessing in that a blessing requests divine aid for protecting the object, while a cleansing is for the purposes of casting out negative energies and influences.

Blessing

When you are blessing a tool, you are requesting Divine assistance to help keep the energies of the tool pure or untainted by undesirable energies. As you bless an object, you are requesting that the tool remain free of evil influences, that it may be used only for positive purposes, and that it be made worthy of use in Magickal applications. The intent of a blessing involves asking that the Divine confer a favorable or desirable quality or condition upon the subject or object of the blessing.

Consecrating

When you consecrate a tool, you are dedicating the tool for a specific purpose, to patron deities, or the Divine in general, often times through the process of a rite, ceremony, or spell. When you consecrate the tool, you make it a sacred object. You literally sanctify the tool so you can use it for specific purposes in religious or Magickal workings. The act of consecrating a tool transforms the item from a mundane object into one that is distinct, hallowed, purified, and sacrosanct. In Magickal workings, consecrating a tool is more powerful than a general blessing; the consecration sanctifies the object thereby making it holy, while a blessing is like a prayer where you request Divine favor or protection for the object/tool.

Charging

To charge an object is to designate the tool for a specific task or purpose. The term *charge* comes from the Old French term *chargier*, meaning, "load," and from *carricāre* meaning, "to carry."[4] Thus, when charging a tool you are Magickally making the object one that carries the duties of the tasks you have assigned to it; the tool subsequently becomes loaded with the work you choose. In addition, the charging further enhances the tool. Like a knight charged with the duty of protecting his king, your tool is charged with the responsibilities you allocate. You can say the following while charging any tool for Magickal use:

Charging Spell

I charge thee (name the tool) *with this task,*
To help in manifesting what I ask,
To extend and expand the reach of my intent,
To focus and concentrate energies sent.

Following the blessing and consecration of the tool/object, the item is ready for you to charge. When you charge an object, you do so through the movement of your will and the use of visualization. Take up the tool in your receptive hand. Hold your projective hand over the tool as you visualize the job/duties/function of the tool. Next, visualize your energy or will moving down your arms, into your hands, and into the object. Continue this process until you intuitively sense the completion of the act.

Anointing

The term anoint comes from the Old French word *enoit* and *oindre* meaning, "to rub on or smear."[5] When you anoint an object, this involves the practice of blessing the object with water or scented oils. During rituals or spells, you can apply oil or water to specific items or you can anoint yourself; for example, you can anoint candles with oils before using them in candle Magick or you can anoint yourself if you are preparing for ritual. You will often need to apply oil or water in a specific direction or in a specific location. In the case of candle Magick, you can draw down universal energies from above or you can push energies outward to force energies in the opposite direction. In the case of self-anointing, you might anoint the third eye before beginning divinatory practices, or you might anoint your body just before you conduct ritual. If you are using oils when anointing something, the scent of the oil should correspond to the Magickal working at hand.

Cleansing, Blessing, Consecrating, Charging, and Anointing

You should cleanse any object or tool before you bless it. In order to cleanse an object, you have to consider the materials used in creating the tool, and you should use the appropriate cleaning materials to physically clean the object. For instance, you should use a metal cleaner to clean objects made of metal or a wood cleaner to clean wooden tools; water can damage some metals or wood. Once you have physically cleansed the tool, you need to cleanse it spiritually as well; you can do this by smudging the object with sage, dragon's blood, or your choice of purifying incense. You can intensify the physical and spiritual cleansing of the object by visualizing any negative energy attached to the object being dispelled or dissipated as you clean the object physically and spiritually.

After cleansing the object, you should bless and consecrate it. You can use a ritual or a spell that allows you to do both processes simultaneously or you can use two separate rituals/spells to achieve the same result. You can use the following blessing/consecration on your Magickal tools and accessories.

Object Blessing and Consecration

To bless and consecrate tools, you will need sage, dragon's blood, frankincense, myrrh, rosemary or other purifying incense, a white or red candle, consecrated water, and sea salt. You can begin the blessing/ consecration by stating your intent aloud. Say:

I seek to bless and consecrate this tool, and I call upon the elements and the Divine to assist me in my endeavor.

Pass the object through the incense smoke. Say:

I bless and consecrate this tool with the element of Air.

Pass the tool a couple of inches over the burning candle, just enough to expose the tool to the heat of the flame, taking considerable care not to burn the tool or yourself. Say:

I bless and consecrate this tool with the element of Fire.

Sprinkle the tool with a little bit of consecrated water. Say:

I bless and consecrate this object/tool with the element of Water.

Sprinkle a little bit of the sea salt on the tool. Say:

I bless and consecrate this tool with the element of Earth.

Hold the tool up high, and speak aloud as you request that the God and Goddess bless and consecrate the object. Express gratitude for the Divine assistance you receive. Finish off the spell blessing/ consecration with:

So mote it be, blessed be.

Anointing an Object

Anointing a tool is not always a necessity, but some practitioners choose to anoint certain tools or themselves when performing rituals. Sometimes, you might anoint candles when preparing for candle Magick. You can anoint your tools if you desire, by choosing an appropriate essential oil. If you are anointing an object that might incur damage if exposed to an oily substance, use consecrated water to anoint the tool.

If you are anointing candles, you can choose an oil that corresponds with the spell or ritual you are about to perform. Apply the oil to the side of the candle with your finger. Move your finger upward from the base of the candle to the candlewick for spells or rites where you are attempting to repel, banish, or move energies away from you. To draw energies and things to you, start at the tip of the candle with the anointing and move your finger in a downward motion from the wick to the candle base. If you are anointing a tool like an athame or wand, start the anointing at the base of the tool and move your finger in an outward motion to the tip. This direction of movement is deliberate; you are applying oil in the same direction that your will and intent moves when the tool is in use.

Binding

The term *bind* can mean to bring things together through the act of tying, but it can also mean to trap, confine, or to place specific limitations on a person, place, or thing. A binding can also involve the act of restricting or confining an individual in order to prevent them from causing harm. Two people can also be bound to one another; in handfastings, the couple's hands are bound together, symbolizing the couple's union. When a person is bound for any reason, you should consider factors concerning free will; bindings on people are usually only performed when necessary and only if the act of binding someone will result in the highest good. For more on the binding process when working with Magick, see the section "Working with Cords" in Chapter 2.

Tips on Choosing Your Magickal Tools

When seeking a Magickal tool, oftentimes, the tool will do the choosing: for example, when wandering around in a store or window-shopping, you might suddenly see or develop an affinity for a tool or you will intuitively know that the tool should and/or will belong to you. For instance, one of the co-authors of this work spotted a gorgeous table in an antique shop and lacked the funds to purchase the table when she spotted it. Nevertheless, the moment that she spotted the table she knew in her heart that the table would one day serve as her Magickal altar. A year later, she returned to the shop and purchased the table where it had remained for over a year. It was as if the tool waited patiently for her to purchase it. The table continues to serve as her altar today. Essentially, if a tool is really the right tool for you, if you ask the Divine for assistance, the Divine will see to it that the tool becomes yours.

If you are in need of a tool and you have not found one that is appealing, it could mean that you have yet to encounter the perfect tool. In this case, you can put a call out to the universe and request that you receive help in finding the tool you desire. If you need a tool and are not sure where to find one or you have found a tool you desire, but require the means to get it, you can use the following "tool calling" spell.

Tool Calling Spell: To Find a New or Lost Tool

Visualize the tool you desire. If you know of the specific tool design that you seek, concentrate on an image of that tool and pay attention to every possible detail as you visualize it. If you know the tool you require, but you have not settled on a style or design, simply concentrate on the type of tool you need. After forming a solid image in your mind's eye, say:

Universe, I ask of thee,
To send the tool I call to me.
Powers above, powers below,
As I request, be it so,
With these words that I speak,
A sacred tool I do seek,
With this spell I will find,
A Magickal tool to make mine.*

***Alternative spell closing:** When you are searching for a lost tool, you can change the final line in the spell to, *"The Magickal tool that is mine."*

If you choose to personalize your tool or to get creative with your tool's design, you are putting your essence or a part of yourself into the tool. Some practitioners feel that handmade or customized tools and objects are more powerful than store-bought items absent of customizations. In addition, if you happen to find an antique tool, bear in mind that any physical changes made to the tool, through painting, decorating, or carving, can diminish the monetary value of the tool in question.

Important Notes on Spells and Rituals

"Thy liquid lyric, rhymed and runed . . . in my heart is softly crooned."
—Clarence Thomas Urmy
"A California Troubadour"

You can use a spell or a ritual to concentrate, focus, raise, and direct your energies and intent toward manifesting a desired result on the physical plane. Spells and rituals include Magickal workings related to protection, defense, abundance, prosperity, and healing. However, a ritual is more ceremonial than most spells, and practitioners often use rituals to honor the Divine, to mark a rite of passage, or to celebrate a specific season, sabbat, or esbat. A spell may be contained within a ritual, but can also stand alone. A spell is the bare bones act of working Magick; it is usually an abbreviated process cutting right to the chase. A ritual incorporates several stages of action/words meant to alter your conscious awareness from mundane to Magickal, invoke deities, guardians, and/or elementals, request divine assistance in mundane/Magickal applications, and it represents a symbolic transformation or initiation. A spell may incorporate some ritual aspects, but it is not as formal as a ritual: this does not mean a spell has a less powerful result when compared to ritual outcomes. While sharing some properties, a spell and a ritual accomplish a similar goal, using two slightly different processes.

Rhyming Format

While it is not always so, many practitioners of Magick use rhyming in their spells. When spells rhyme, it lends a musical sound to the poetic verse spoken. Rhyming spells also have a unique rhythm, thereby creating a different energy than words that, when spoken or written, do not rhyme. The rhyme and cadence of spells allows you to build up a rhythmic intensity as you accumulate energies to back your spell work. In addition, if you want to memorize a spell or ritual so that you do not have to read it off a piece of paper or out of a book, it is far easier to memorize something that rhymes. Once you memorize a spell, you can focus on the importance of what you are saying instead of trying to remember what words you need to say.

Everyday Common Sense

Before you make use of any of the following spells or rituals shared in this book, it is only fair to provide you with a word of caution. Common sense is one of the most basic and important tools you will ever have, not only in Magickal applications, but also in life in general. To that end, do not forgo actions involving basic common sense just because you performed a spell or ritual. For example, when you do a spell to protect your home, it does not mean you are free to leave the windows and doors unlocked when you are not at home! Doing so is just tempting the Fates and waiting for trouble to happen!

The use of Magick requires focused energy, beyond the typical exertion applied in day-to-day tasks. Before you perform a spell, consider if it is worth the energy to perform a spell and then to ignore your own common sense. There is little use in summoning the aid of the Divine or performing spells to get you out of a bind or situation where a bit of planning, practicality, and sensibility could have helped you avoid potential problems in the first place. Not using common sense always backfires in everyday life and when working Magick. If you rely on Magick alone, you leave a lot to chance. Magickal practices should never take the place of the sound daily practices one would use to manage his or her affairs; rather, Magick should supplement the use of common sense in every situation.

Intent

Magick is not black; it is not white, and it is not gray; Magick remains neutral and is defined entirely by the practitioner's intent. The energies you put forth in any Magickal working will shape the outcome; what you put forth is what you get in return. Your intent must be steadfast, strong, and well focused for Magickal practices to work. Without a clear intent, any spell you cast, regardless of the witty, clever way it is written/performed, at minimum, will have a weakened result, or it will not work at all. At worst, if a spell is lacking in intent, it can backfire on you. You manifest your intent through the thoughts, words, tools, and actions that you use when spell casting. If your intent is weak, you will have a weakened result.

After you perform a ritual or spell, you should never cast doubt on the fact that your Magick will work. Doubting your Magick slams the door on the possibility of manifestation. You must be positive about your Magickal workings, know exactly what it is you are trying to achieve, and you must accept without any uncertainty that it will occur.

Specificity

Being specific with words and actions allows you to focus your intent with greater clarity. Haphazardly working Magick can prove disastrous and it will definitely influence the outcome of your Magickal workings. For instance, imagine working a spell so that you can find a new job.

When you write the spell and perform it, imagine that you have only focused on finding a new job, and you have not specified that you want a job that will match your skills, provide a solid income, or make you content. Following the spell, you might indeed find a job opportunity, but the job might prove boring or you might land a position that does not pay very well. Even worse, if you did not specify that you wanted a job opportunity where you would be content or satisfied, you can end up with a job that makes you miserable.

As you conduct your spells or rituals, you should do so with the intent to harm none. Envision conducting a spell to find work, then finding your dream job, only to discover that it was at the expense of a close friend or another person who had suddenly lost the position, thereby creating the ideal circumstances to make the job available to you. The importance of proper wording in spells cannot be overemphasized. Imagine conducting a spell to end a conflict in a relationship, but that you do not define the conflict or the type of resolution you seek. Now consider the relationship coming to a sudden and abrupt end after you perform the spell; your conflict is resolved, but not necessarily in the way you may have imagined.

As you specify meaning through the word choices you make, also take into account that many words have two or more meanings; what a word connotes and what you actually mean can be two different things: Ambiguity can weaken spell results or produce chaotic, undependable outcomes in spell workings. You will also need a clear awareness of potential outcomes when working Magick. For example, if you write a spell and perform it and the words you have chosen can result in more than one outcome, you might not get the precise outcome you expect, no matter how aligned your actions are. You will need to put some forethought into the different outcomes a spell might produce before you perform any Magickal application at all.

While the power of intent and the level of clarity you use when expressing your intent dictates spell results, the subconscious also wields power, and can influence the outcome of your work. It is therefore not only imperative that you specify your intent in all Magickal workings, but that you are equally aware of things on a subconscious level. For instance, if you are seeking a new job and you conduct a spell to get one, but on a subconscious level you feel that you are not deserving of the position or you lack the skills to fulfill the job in question, the subconscious thoughts you are having can weaken the effect of your Magickal working. When it comes to Magickal applications, spells, and rituals, you need to have your conscious mind, intent, and subconscious aligned so that you can achieve the outcome you desire.

Personalizing Spells and Rituals

Although you can use any of the spells or rituals offered in this book, you will often find that spells/rituals are far more effective if you create them yourself; self-written spells come from the heart, thus, they reflect your creativity and your Magickal intent far greater than the words of a spell written by another. When you write a spell or adapt one for your own purposes, you are using words, symbols, concepts, archetypes, and psychological constructs that are meaningful to you. When writing your own spells, it lends additional power to the Magickal application: your power, intent, and desire.

If you do decide to write or adapt spells/rituals that you have gotten from other sources, you need to make sure the spells/rites are extremely specific. Your intent must precisely match the words and actions you convey. If you find rites or spells that contain words or chants that you are not sure of, refrain from using the spell/rite until you know its exact meaning. When you are not sure about what you are saying, not only can you not empower the words or chants with the appropriate amount of emotion or intent, you may be asking for something you do not want at all. Knowing the proper pronunciation of words is equally important in Magickal workings; the specific sounds that words create are Magickal too.

Chapter 1
Altar Tools

"An altar in life, alters our life."
—H. H. Swami Tejomayananda

The Altar
Description, Uses, and Symbolism

An altar is a structure commonly placed in the center or at the heart of an established sacred space. The term *altar* comes from the Latin *altāre* meaning "high place."[1] It typically has a flat surface where Magickal tools are stored, displayed, and used. The altar serves as a physical focal point in ritual worship and Magickal workings.

An altar can be round, square, rectangular or octagonal in shape, and the structure can and should be made of natural materials like wood, stone, or glass. On top of the altar, you can arrange your tools according to the cardinal direction and element the tool is associated with; the size of the altar is of no consequence, but you should consider the amount of space that you have in the room where the altar is established. You will also want to reflect on the size of the tools you own or will be purchasing in the future to ensure that you have enough room on your altar for everything you want to place on it.

Round tables are the preferred type of table for an altar; practitioners of Feng Shui believe that a round table allows for the free flow of positive energies or chi. Round tables lack hard curves and lines, so it allows for a unification of energies. The altar represents your spiritual center, the self, and it is set in a location that you identify as sacred space. As you establish an area or sacred place, the location will be a spot where you will begin to return to repeatedly: a site that will instantly invoke an altered state of awareness. The altar is a reminder of the reverence you have for the Divine, and it acts as a mirror, reflecting your inner emotions and intentions in the outer world. During rituals, the altar is at the center of a "between" place. It helps to invoke an atmosphere of reverence, and it represents, not only the Divine, but a mirror image of the inner self or spirit. If it is in the shape of a circle, it can represent the cycle of life, death, and rebirth. No matter what shape your altar is, it is representative of the four elements: Air, Fire, Water, and Earth, Akasha (the combination of all elements), and the four cardinal directions: East, South, West, and North. As time passes, and you use the altar repeatedly for Magickal workings, spell casting, and rituals, the altar accumulates positive Magickal energies with every use.

You can use your altar for the purposes of working Magick, paying reverence to the Divine, and during ritual workings; however, you can also use an altar as a place to make offerings to the God and Goddess. In coven workings, the group may gather around the altar during ritual or solitary practitioners will often stand in front of the altar. In either case, the altar is facing North since it is the cardinal direction associated with power. An altar can also be set up in a sacred space where one returns every time they want to evoke a feeling of reverence, and you can have more than one altar if you desire.

Altars can be established indoors or out. You can even create a portable altar that you can take with you when traveling. The altar can hold and store your Magickal tools. In the case of a portable altar, choose a sizeable bag to carry all of your tools in or store all of your most important tools in a box that you can carry along with you.

Making it Magickal

Once you have selected a structure for your Magickal altar, do not use it for mundane purposes of any kind; for example, if you choose an old dining room table to use as an altar, do not later use it for sitting while eating dinner! After choosing the structure you desire, you will need to use a compass to find out what the cardinal directions are so you can position your altar facing the cardinal direction of North. You will need to cleanse and consecrate the altar before using it for Magickal workings. After you clean and consecrate the altar, you can decorate it with different colored altar cloths or decorative elements as well as set up your Magickal tools and/or statues. You can embellish the altar according to the season, the sabbat, to your color preference, or you can use colors specifically aligned with a Magickal working that you plan on performing.

Care, Maintenance, and Cautions

As mentioned earlier, your altar is a representation of you and your Divine reverence; you will therefore want to keep the structure clean and organized: Consider keeping it clean as an act of tremendous import. You will want to clean the altar by choosing the appropriate cleaning materials for the structure you choose; how often you clean your altar is totally up to you, but you will want to have the area perfected before each Magickal working. You will want to wash your altar cloths regularly, following the care instructions for the material; this will help to keep any damage occurring to flame retardant materials.

You will also want to re-consecrate your altar any time you feel it is necessary to do so. If someone has been near your altar and you feel that the individual has somehow tainted the energies of the structure, re-consecrate it. You can set up a schedule for cleaning your altar just before every esbat (full moon) or consecrating it before every sabbat (High Holy Day).

Your altar should be in a safe place where visitors, children, or pets will not disturb it. If you use altar cloths, make sure that they do not hang too low to the floor; long, flowing altar cloths can prove dangerous as you move around the altar. Your altar must be sturdy and capable of handling significant weight to hold all of your tools, statues, and other Magickal items. If the altar is made of glass, make sure the glass is durable enough to sustain plenty of weight.

For the Crafty Witch

If you are establishing an outdoor altar, you can use a picnic table (if you do not plan to use it for family gatherings), a tree stump, a flat surfaced rock, or a marble bench. Large wooden spools used for holding electrical wiring can also make handy outdoor altars. If you are creating an indoor altar, you can use a small coffee table, a small dresser, or even an old trunk as an altar for your sacred objects. Your altar does not have to be ultra expensive. If you find that you eventually outgrow the size of your altar, you can always upgrade to a larger size when you have the additional space.

You have tremendous freedom when you are personalizing your altar. Consider using fabric paints to add designs to altar cloths or wood burning tools to add decorative elements to your altar's surface. If your altar is made of wood, you can sand down the altar, stain or paint it, or consider using a glue gun to fill in the wood-burned images with a line of glitter. If you like mosaic patterns, you can also add mosaic tiles to the altar's surface. You might even want to decorate the surface of your altar with silk flowers, peacock feathers, seashells, or crystals.

Athame and Sword

Description, Uses, and Symbolism

The athame is a double-edged ceremonial knife, sometimes called a ritual dagger. The pronunciation of *athame* remains highly disputed, but common pronunciations include *ah-thame, ath-may, ah-tha-may, ath-ah-me,* and *awe-thame*. Some athames have a black handle or hilt, while others sport decorative handles made of various metals or wood. The blade can be sharpened or unsharpened. The sword is larger than the athame, but serves similar purposes when used in Magickal applications; you may or may not have enough room on your altar for a sword, depending upon your altar's size.

The athame is like a small sword; the instrument is fire-forged, and it is therefore associated with the Fire element as well as the South. This tool serves as an extension of you, and you will use it for directing energies and intentions. Do not use the sharp edges of an athame for cutting anything physically. The athame's blade symbolically represents the sharp and urgent qualities of drive, passion, strength of mind, and the rapid movement of will. The athame allows you to draw Magickal energies from within, to pierce through the mundane plane, and to push your intentions into/through the physical for the purposes of manifesting desires.

Athames and swords can be used for the purposes of cutting cords of energetic attachment, circle casting, cutting Magickal doorways after a circle has been cast, for cutting away negative energies, and this ritual blade can be used to direct your personal energies in ritual and Magickal applications. In Magickal workings, use the athame to "cut away" undesirable dysfunctions, confusions, or for Magickally cutting through perceived realities in order to penetrate different realms for the purposes of obtaining spiritual guidance or wisdom. You can even use the athame to write symbols in the air while performing a rite/spell, thereby intensifying the visualization, meaning, and influential energies of the symbols you use. As you use the athame, your will moves down your arm, into the athame, and out the tip of the blade, so you will literally empower the symbols you create with your personal power. When used in Magick, the tool helps focus energies and to send the current of energy outward toward a desired result. Using an athame allows you to control energies or draw them down in Magickal applications too; for example, a practitioner that uses an athame during the Lesser Banishing Ritual of the Pentagram uses the tool to draw down universal energies and to control their direction.

The athame or sword is phallic-like in design and is therefore representative of the Divine Masculine. This tool connotes active and projective qualities, or God forces. The act of placing the athame's blade into the Chalice during ritual proves symbolic of the Great Rite or the Great Marriage of the God and Goddess. Athames are associated with the astrological signs of Aries, and Scorpio, and the planet Mars, thereby linking athames to practices involving Magickal self-defense.

Making it Magickal

Once you choose an athame or sword, you have to bless, cleanse, and consecrate the tool before using it for Magickal purposes. You should place the athame in the South on your altar due to its fiery associations. Many witchcraft traditions prohibit exposure of the athame to any kind of blood since doing so taints the tool thereby making it unsuitable for Magickal workings. If the athame is tainted, replace it by burying it and buying a new one. By burying the tool, you can allow the negative energies to drain into the earth to dissipate.

Care, Maintenance, and Cautions

Always keep your athame or sword clean and free of debris. When not in use, leave it in the sheath to protect the blade. You can clean the blade with a metal cleaner. Consider the materials used in the creation of the athame or sword's hilt as well, and tend to it accordingly.

This tool should be kept away from children, pets, or anyone that could wind up harming themselves with it; remember to keep your tools in a safe area, and away from others who may not respect them as much as you do. Keep your athame away from people who might emit negative energies: The energies can attach to the tool, and you will have to cleanse as well as consecrate it before using it again. Finally, never carelessly wave an athame or sword around in the air or allow someone who is incapable of respecting the tool to handle it.

For the Crafty Witch

If you cannot afford an athame, a kitchen knife is an inexpensive alternative: One that can serve as your athame until you can afford a better tool. You can also use a decorative letter opener for the same purposes. Just remember that whatever item you choose, you can no longer use it for mundane applications.

If you have chosen an athame with a plain black or wooden handle, you can decorate the handle with Magickal symbols, meaningful runes, or stones, gems, and materials that appeal to you. Just make sure that the materials you choose are non-flammable and that the materials do not interfere with your ability to hold the handle of the athame when it is in use. As you are decorating the tool, take care that you do not accidentally cut yourself with the blade while you are handling it.

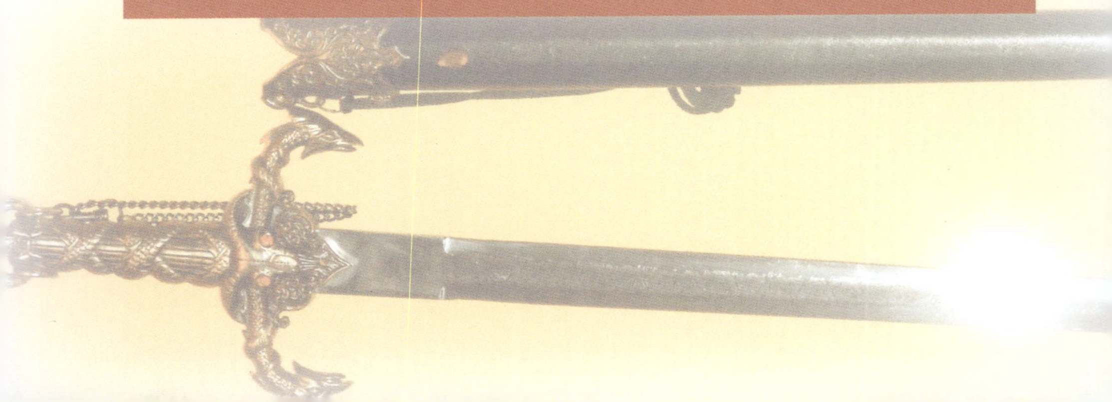

Bell

Description, Uses, and Symbolism

A bell is a percussion instrument, sometimes called a "hand-bell," available in various sizes and shapes containing a mallet affixed inside a dome. When someone shakes or moves the bell, it will create a specific sound influenced by the size of the tool and the materials used in its construction. A bell can create many unique sounds; some offer light, chime-like tones while others have heavy, thick sounds like cowbells.

Bells are made of ceramic, glass, brass, silver, steel, iron, wood, bamboo, or alternative materials. Various cultures including the Assyrians, Egyptians, Indians, Celts, Chinese, Japanese, Africans, Greeks, and Romans have used bells for Magickal applications. Archeologists found nearly eighty tiny bronze bells, along with other objects, at a dig in Nimroud, an ancient Assyrian city now known as Mosul, Iraq—the bells were contained inside two ancient copper cauldrons.[2] The ancient Egyptians sometimes buried the deceased with bells, and like the sistrum, would use bells to create a tone, thereby stirring up stagnant energies in order to drive away evil forces or demons.[3] Bells were also used to announce the commencement of Osirian festivals.[4] Bells are even parts of priestly garb described in the Book of Exodus. When making the "ephod" or robe for Aaron, the hem of the robe was lined with pomegranates and alternating bells;[5] thus, when the robe was worn, the bells would announce the presence of the High Priest.

Small hand bells were in use in England during the late thirteenth century; at the time, bells could weigh up to seven pounds.[6] Before the reformation, small bells were sounded for the purposes of denoting a time for prayer and to "clear a passage" for the dead as the deceased was brought to the burial site.[7] Today, the bell is still used in Magickal workings. It should be small enough to place on the altar. The tone, shape, design, and color vary upon preference. The bell chosen should be light, practical, and easily portable. When choosing audible qualities, the tone is considerably important: The sound that the bell produces should be pleasing, but not overly obtrusive.

Symbolically, the ringing of a bell during ritual practices represents the extension of your will and intent; as the bell rings, its sound breaks through the invisible barrier between the physical and the Magickal realms/astral planes. The sound of the bell induces a ripple effect: As the sound expands and travels, it carries the intent of the Magickal worker with it outward and in every direction. The sounding of the bell is also a trigger for your subconscious and helps in inducing a higher state of consciousness for ritual and Magickal applications. In Magickal workings, the ringing bell is a method for connecting with spiritual beings and it serves as an invitation to protective spirits and guardians. Since the bell is associated with the element of Air, it is a symbol of communication and change, and because it is associated with the cardinal direction of the East, the bell is symbolic of new beginnings.

The physical nature of the bell is representative of the God and Goddess or the dual nature of the Divine. The handle is phallic-like, and the dome shaped bottom of the bell is womb-shaped. Interestingly, the bell is much like a mini, inverted chalice: a tool that also represents the dual nature and the union of the Divine. The word *bell*, as a verb, also signifies the sound that a stag makes during the rutting season to attract or call to a mate;[8] the latter meaning may subtly connote the Great Rite and the connection between the Goddess and Her consort, the Stag King.

Making it Magickal

You can choose any bell that appeals to you for use in Magickal workings, just make sure that it is pleasing to the eye, easy to use, and that you appreciate its sound quality. Consider the metal or alternative material used in creating the bell: a silver bell will hold Goddess/lunar energies, while a bronze bell is specifically associated with the Goddess Venus. Meanwhile, gold, iron, or brass bells are associated with solar deities. You will need to convert the bell into a Magickal tool by blessing, charging, and consecrating it. Emphasis is on the idea of converting the tool, since once prepared for Magickal uses, it will not be used for mundane purposes in the future.

Care, Maintenance, and Cautions

You should care for the bell only after considering the materials used in its construction. If it is metal, use a metal cleaner to keep the bell looking beautiful. If it is made of glass, you can use a mild detergent or dish liquid and warm water to free the tool of dust or debris. If it is made of wood, the bell can be cleaned with a gentle wood cleaner. Keeping the bell clean is important because an accumulation of dust cannot only affect the bell's aesthetic qualities, it can alter the tone of the bell, even if only slightly. If you decide to store the bell until you are ready to use it, wrap it in a small black cloth to keep the positive energies in and the negative energies out.

To protect your bell, make sure you keep it from falling into negative or undesirable hands. If a person inadvertently touches your tool without your consent, re-consecrate it and charge it with positive energies. If you place your bell on an elevated table or stand, make sure it is not too close to the edge of the table; if it falls from a great height, the fall can damage it.

For the Crafty Witch

If you do not have a bell, you can use a gong or singing bowl; bear in mind the latter tools may cause issues with portability. You can often find tiny bells sold in a dollar store. You can find some beautiful bells at garage sales and flea markets too. If you buy a bell from a flea market or a thrift store, you can take it home, polish it, and make it look brand new. If you make ceramics, get a bisque bell, clean it, have it fired, and use copper wire to attach a hammer to the dome's interior. If the bell has a long handle you can decorate the handle with leather, suede, copper wiring, ribbon, or you can add small beads to the bottom rim of the bell to make it more attractive.

Boline

Description, Uses, and Symbolism

Boline is sometimes spelled as *bolleen, boleen,* or *bolline*. The term *boline* may come from the word *bowline*, thus describing the bowed or "bent and arching" line of the knife's blade.[9] The term *boline* also comes from the Italian term *bollino* or *borino*: terms used to describe the "chisel or pounce used by a professional engraver."[10] You can use this tool for harvesting flowers, herbs, thin pieces of wood, and some practitioners use it as a hook that they can place into the earth. This tool can be for uprooting and transplanting plants, but you can also use it for the purposes of creating large outdoor Magickal circles since it can hold fast a cord for circle casting purposes. The modern boline hosts a crescent or sickle-shaped blade. You can use the modern boline for the cutting of flowers and herbs. The tool should be sharp enough to cut through thick stems, roots, and plant materials with ease.

It is important to note that the appropriate use of a boline is debatable; some Witches only use a boline for cutting plants and herbs, while others use it for cutting small pieces of wood, carving symbols in candle wax, cord cutting, or inscribing objects with Magickal words, ciphers, or runes. If you are going to go beyond the act of using a boline for harvesting plants, flowers, and herbs, you might be better off with a straight blade knife compared to the crescent-moon shaped blade found on traditional bolines; you can more easily use the point of a straight blade for carving purposes. You might find that a straight edged boline also comes in handy if you decide to make your own candles.

While many Witches prefer a white-handled or wooden boline, there are bolines made with alternative materials that can serve you equally well. Many practitioners insist on having a boline with a white handle; this creates a sense of balance if one owns a black-handled athame. It is interesting to note that the athame, a tool only used for the act of symbolic cutting, is the direct opposite of a boline, a tool used for cutting objects in a physical manner. By distinguishing the use of the athame and the boline, the Witch has two tools that end up representing the astral and physical realms as well as the act of working within both planes of existence. Some bolines have straight handles made of various metals, and others have curved or partially curved handles made out of natural wood or bone. You can also find bolines that have decorative, engraved blades and handles.

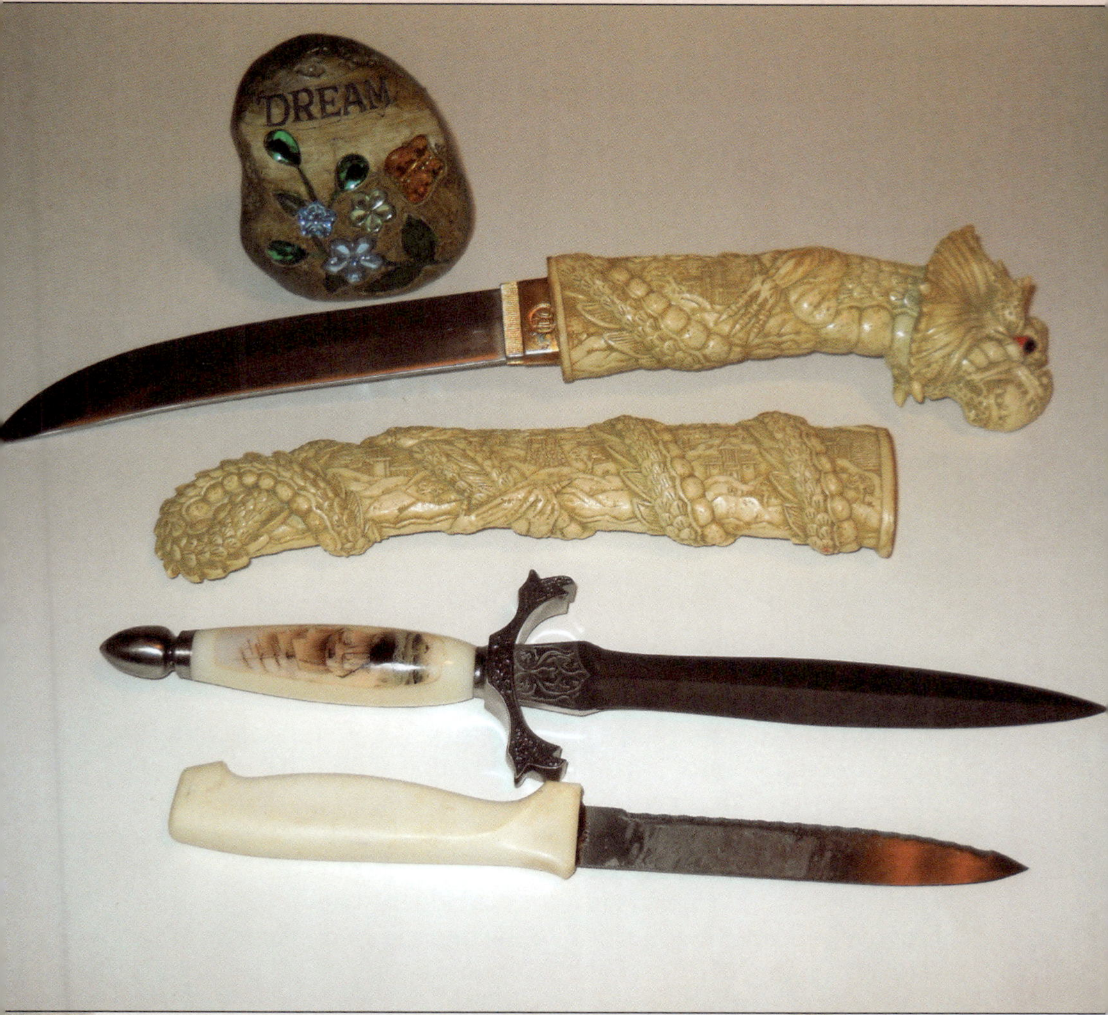
DREAM

Making it Magickal

Once you choose a boline, cleanse, bless, consecrate, and charge it. When not in use, leave it on your altar or store it away in a safe place. If you decide to store it, keep it in a sheath as well as a black cloth to keep negative energies from attaching to the tool.

Care, Maintenance, and Cautions

If you buy a boline with a sheath, make sure you store it in its proper covering. If you decide to travel with the boline, always keep the sheath on the blade until you are ready to use the tool. Whether you choose a straight or curved boline, the blade will have to be very sharp in order for the tool to prove useful. Be considerably careful as you cut plants. You should always use the edge of the boline facing away from you when you are cutting with it; never draw the boline toward you when you are cutting anything. In some traditions, like the athame, exposure to blood taints the boline. When tainted, bury the tool in the earth and replace it with a new one.

For the Crafty Witch

You can use a straight edged, white-handled kitchen knife to serve as a boline. If you have a boline with a handle made of wood, you can carve or burn Magickal symbols or the name of the tool into the handle. You may want to do some practice designs on paper before you begin engraving the actual handle of the boline. If burned or engraved deeply enough, you can line the hollowed out portion of the design, symbol, or writings with a thin line of glue. Then add your choice of colored glitter to the decorative additions. You might want to apply a coat of polyurethane when finished to keep the design and glitter intact. As with your athame, you can decorate the handle with gems, stones, and other decorative embellishments, but you will need to make sure that the ornamentations do not hinder your ability to grip the knife's hilt firmly.

Candles

Description, Uses, and Symbolism

Candles are a means of generating light via a structure made of wax and alternative materials. Candle flames are symbolic of solar energies. Candles vary in size, style, design, materials, and color. You can use any type of candle for Magickal workings including pillars, tapers, jar candles, votives, tea lights, gel candles, luminarias, floating candles, or specialty candles. Some candles have a single wick and others have more than one. The most popular kinds of candles used in Magickal applications, however, are pillar, taper, tea light, and votive varieties. When you place candles on an altar, they mark the cardinal directions and therefore represent East, South, West, and North. Candles also represent the elements, elementals, and guardians. You can use them during rituals, spells, meditation, when working candle Magick, scrying, or when banishing negative energies.

Candles are not only fire tools, but they fall under the category of Akashic tools as well; thus, they embody all of the elements combined. The wax represents the earth, the flame represents fire; the melting wax represents the element of water, and the smoke from the flame as well as the energies the candle emits represents the element of Air. On the altar, both the color and the positioning of the candle are relevant to the candle's application. In general, candles are associated with the element of Fire. However, white and yellow candles in the East signify Air; red candles in the South signify Fire; blue candles in the West signify water, and brown or green candles in the North signify Earth. A purple candle on the altar represents the combination of all the elements or Akasha. You can use black candles for the purposes of absorbing negative energies and white candles for emitting positive energies. You can also use gold and silver candles to represent the masculine and feminine Divine.

You can use candles to illuminate darkness: this is true in a mundane and Magickal sense. The flame of candles represent the spark of life, the passion, fire, or spark behind Magickal workings, as well as the fiery nature of inspiration and creativity. You can charge candles with specific Magickal purposes; when burned, the candle color and charge allow you to release your desires into the universe. Even after you extinguish a candle, the energies and intentions continue to project on an astral level.

Color	Direction	Signifying
Yellow and White	East →	Air
Red	South ↓	Fire
Blue	West ←	Water
Brown and Green	North ↑	Earth

Purple: combination of all the elements or Akasha
Black: absorbing negative energies
White: emitting positive energies
Gold and Silver: the masculine and feminine Divine

Making It Magickal

You can get candles for very little expense at your local store or you can order them online. Some practitioners choose to make candles; the belief is that by making the candles you make them more powerful by empowering them with your personal energies. It is a common practice to make candles around the time of Candlemas (Imbolc – February 1 and 2) each year; this is the season the represents new beginnings, the first stirrings of spring, and is considered the best time to restock one's cabinet with Magickal tools, items, and accessories. When using candles, consecrate and charge them before use. As mentioned earlier, you can anoint candles with specific oils that correspond with a Magickal application.

Care, Maintenance, and Cautions

Make sure you use the appropriate candleholders when burning candles; attempts to put a large candle in a holder that is too small can break the candle or can cause the candle topple over when it is in use. Likewise, if you use a large candleholder with a small candle, again you run the risk of having the candle topple over. Keep candles out of areas where there is excessive heat and/or sunlight too; sunlight can cause them to fade in color and over time, can cause the candles to melt. Do not leave a burning candle untended. Make sure the area where the candle is burning is far enough away from anything flammable. Candles should remain out of reach of children and pets. When burning candles, place each candle on a solid, stable, non-flammable, or flame-retardant surface. If using candles during ritual workings and spell casting, beware of free flowing arm sleeves, robes, attire, and long hair, especially if you use hair spray.

For the Crafty Witch

If you do not have the specific color candle you need to perform a Magickal working, in a pinch, a white candle will work well. The notion that white candles work as a substitute for any other colored candle is based upon the principle that the color white, as a sound wave, is the mixture of all colors, and as a light wave, it is the absence of color; this means you can Magickally charge the candle to be any color you desire. If you have a tight budget, you can collect candle wax that has burned off from other candles and recycle the wax to make new candles.

When carving runes or symbols in candles, align your Magickal intentions with the symbols/runes you create. If you make your own candles, add things like Magickal herbs, shells, glitter, or other materials that give the candle a unique appearance and deeper Magickal significance. Adding your choice of scented oils can also intensify the Magickal properties of the candles you make. Bear in mind that some objects, when put inside candles, may affect the way the candles burn.

Make your own candles at home using a double boiler system or two pots. Add water to one pot and the wax to the other; place the pot containing the wax over the pot with water in it. Once heated, the steam will rise and melt the wax in the uppermost pot. To add color to white wax, melt a few crayons or add a few drops of dye into the mix. With a wooden spoon, stir the mixture to make the color consistent. Recycle old metal tea light holders or use a mini/large muffin tin to make new candles. Spraying the pan with a non-stick spray makes it easier to remove candles from the tin. Position the wicks in the middle of each holder, pour the wax in, and allow the wax to cool. If any of the candles stick to the tin, you can place the tin in your freezer: this will help loosen up the wax so you can remove them.

If you desire, you can make rolled taper candles from sheets of beeswax or by dipping a long wick into a long, tall metal container of melted wax, allowing the wax to cool, and repeating the process; bear in mind that this process is time consuming, thereby requiring a lot of patience. There are also candle-making kits you can buy; you can find tart molds, dyes, scents, wick tabs, wicks, lidded jars, and wax blocks at your local craft store.

Censer, Thurible, and Incense

Description, Uses, and Symbolism

The term Thurible (pronounced *thur-ah-bul*) refers to a fireproof vessel: one you can use to contain burning incense. In rituals or during spell casting, the person that carries the thurible is a Thurifer (pronounced *thur-ah-fer*):[11] a term stemming from the Latin meaning "the bearer of the incense." This tool can be made of a variety of materials including shells, clay, brass, glass, metal, or wood.

A simple censer is made of brass or an alternative precious metal and is a small, short vessel. Sometimes the lid is pointed, but there are censers that have flat tops. The lid contains several holes on it to allow the smoke from the burning incense to rise out of the censer. Some censers are more ornate and have several chains from which they are suspended; this type of censer allows the carrier to swing the censer back and forth in order to force the emitting scent in all directions.

For centuries and in a variety of cultures, censers and incense have served as religious tools. Ancient Jewish priests would use censers as a method of making an offering to God when they were in the holy sanctuary. Today, priests in Roman Catholic churches use censers during mass. In Magickal practices, the scent of incense conjures up an altered state of awareness during meditations allowing you to get into the appropriate mindset for worship, ritual workings, meditations, and spell casting work.

Some practitioners use incense smoke as it escapes the censer for the purposes of divination: *capnomancy, kapnomancy, knissomancy, livanomancy,* or *libanomancy* are terms defining the practice of divining by smoke. Capnomancy or kapnomancy is derived from the Greek *kapnós* meaning smoke, and *manteia* meaning divination.[12] In ancient times, capnomancy involved the process of divining from the smoke that rose up off a burning sacrifice; if the smoke was heavy and hung in the air, it served as a bad omen, but if the smoke rose up straight, swift, and proved light, then it was considered a good sign.[13] Knissomancy or livanomancy is divination done specifically through burning the incense of your choosing and reading the smoke that rises from it.[14] Alternatively, libanomancy is a form of divination involving the use of frankincense.[15] Knissomancy, libanomancy, and livanomancy not only include the act of interpreting how the smoke rises from burning incense, but also sometimes involves the act of reading the fallen ashes for omens and signs. Tupramancy, tephramancy, and spodomancy are divination practices involving the act of reading ashes after burning incense; the practice is traced to pagan Rome when priests would use the ashes for making predictions.[16] The practice of using incense in divinatory practices remains in use, even today.

When choosing incenses, align the scent you choose with deities or your personal will. Incense serves as the "breath of life" in Magickal workings; you can use it to summon the power of wind or Air, summon guardian spirits, and clear/cleanse a space for sacred Magickal workings. The scent of the incense you choose creates an ambiance that will help prepare your mind for Magickal workings, relaxation, grounding, and meditation. The use of incense allows the scent to penetrate the barriers between the realm of Magick and the physical as well.

Incense smoke represents prayers or spells and their ascension upward where one's prayers/spells can be divinely addressed or answered by the universe. Sometimes incense is burned as an offering to the God and Goddess to thank them for blessings, Divine guidance, or for requesting their assistance with a Magickal working or a mundane issue. Incense smoke also represents the movement of your personal will. Incense is associated with the element of Air, the East, new beginnings, and/or communication. The burning incense carries energies and intent through the air, across the planes and expresses the intent of the practitioner, absent of limitations or boundaries. The smoke rising up from the incense is symbolic of the veil between the worlds: a veil that is pierced or lifted during Magickal rites.

Making it Magickal

When buying a censer, keep in mind that other people have handled the tool before you have; this means there may or may not be some undesirable energies connected to your tool. Cleanse, bless, consecrate, and charge the censer before use. Position the censer in the eastern corner of your altar to align it with the appropriate energies. Part of what makes your censer a Magickal tool is what you burn inside of it. Choose incense based upon Magickal correspondences associated with specific scents.

Care, Maintenance, and Cautions

To ensure the purity of the scent produced by the incense placed in an enclosed censer it is imperative that you keep the censer clean. If you really want the metals to shine on the censer you will want to have clean hands before you clean or handle it; the oils on your hands can transfer to the surface of your censer and make it more difficult to clean. How you care for your censer will depend on the materials used in its construction: if it is made of metal, you can use a metal cleaner. If you use a product that is flammable, you will want to make sure that you thoroughly remove any of the remaining cleaner before you burn incense in the censer. Clean metal censers with a teaspoon of ammonia diluted in warm water. Soak the censer for two or three minutes before removing it from the water. Make sure that the censer is completely dry after washing it. Be aware that you will probably not be able to get rid of any burnt soot marks on the inside of the censer; this is of no consequence since you will be using the censer repeatedly for burning incense.

If you use a wooden incense holder, simply remove any remaining ashes and wipe the wooden holder clean with a dry cloth. Do not use oil-based cleaners. When you have a censer with precious or semiprecious stones, make sure to keep any metal cleaner away from the stones and only use an appropriate cleaner for the stones in your thurible or censer. Meanwhile, if you have chosen an abalone shell as an incense burner, empty the shell of ashes, soak it in soap and water, and gently dry the shell. If you want to restore some of the sheen of the mother of pearl-like surface inside, put a couple drops of Vitamin E oil on the shell and rub it in with a dry cloth. Make sure you wipe off as much of the excess oil as possible.

Some censers are made of soapstone; clean this type of tool with dish detergent and warm water. Never use steel wool or other scratchy cleaning products on soapstone; the stone is soft and porous: abrasive cleaning materials will damage the surface. If you want to keep the exterior of the soapstone censer attractive, you can apply a bit of Vitamin E oil or mineral oil to the exterior to help make the soapstone maintain its attractiveness. If working with a clay censer, simply rinse the tool off with some warm water.

Never walk away from burning incense or leave it untended. If you are using a censer that does not have an enclosed body and lid, use something appropriate to catch falling ashes. If you choose a thurible with chains, use care to ensure that the chains do not tangle when it is in use. If you desire, purchase a stand so you can hang or suspend the thurible when you store it. Additionally, the stand helps to keep the censer away from flammable objects. If you lift and carry the thurible during ritual or spell workings, make sure you have a good grip on the tool so you do not drop it. The same goes for passing the censer to another practitioner; if you are doing Magickal workings with someone else and there is a need to pass the censer back and forth, make sure the person you pass the censer to has a firm hold on it before you let go.

If you have a small tabletop censer with a metal lid, make sure the censer has had sufficient time to cool down before you attempt to open the lid, to remove the ashes, or to replace the burnt incense inside; censers with metal lids become hot quickly and can lead to unwanted burns. Some censers are equipped with chains on the metal lid; you can use the chain to gently pull the lid of the censer to open if it is still hot; take care not to pull too hard on the chain to prevent tipping the censer over. Always let any burnt incense cool off inside the censer's chamber. When positioning a censer, make sure it is not near windows, in a drafty area, or near curtains.

If using a censer that allows you to use coals to ignite an incense cone, position the coal evenly at the bottom of the inside of the censer so that it can burn correctly. Place the incense on top and in the middle of the burning coal. The coal has to be lit before you position the incense on it; you will therefore want to use tongs or tweezers to place the cone in the correct position and to prevent burns. If you are using granular incense, you can use a spoon to place a small amount of the incense on the burning coal.

For the Crafty Witch

If you do not have a censer, you can use a candle to hold a stick of incense while it burns. You can gently force the end of the incense stick into the wax of a pillar candle until the incense is stable enough to light and burn. You can also use cone incense in a glass ashtray covered with aluminum foil; the foil helps to protect the ashtray from overheating. You can use a large seashell as an incense burner too; in fact, you can purchase an abalone shell incense holder. You can also get an inexpensive incense holder made of wood. Stands for thuribles can prove very expensive, so if you want to save on money, you can invest in one or more hooks that you can mount to the wall in your home, or even position in the ground outside for outdoor rituals.

If you are practicing Magick outdoors, you can place an incense stick in the earth instead of using a censer. If you want to burn an incense cone outdoors, you can use the metal container from an old tea light candle. You can also use votive candleholders: fill up the holder three quarters of the way with sand that can hold both cones and sticks.

You have the option of using oil burners for heating scented oils. This tool often has a small bowl on top of a wide pedestal with an opening for inserting a tea light. Add water and a few drops of oil into the burner's bowl. When the tea light heats the oil and water mixture, the scent rises up into the air. Monitor an oil burner carefully: as the water and oil heats up, it also evaporates. When necessary, add more of the oil and water mixture. If you fail to add more of the mixture in a timely manner, you run the risk of having the burner break or crack from overheating.

To make a homemade censer or incense holder out of clay, shape the clay into any form you desire and allow it to harden. Paint your creation using acrylic paints. Put a gloss coat on your handmade incense holder so it is easier to clean or dust in the future. If you are familiar with making ceramics, your ceramic figurines can make great incense holders too. Find a bisque figure that appeals to you and before you fire it, place a small hole in an easily accessible area where you can later insert a stick of incense. Make measurements to ensure that the stick has plenty of burning room so you do not expose the ceramic figurine or statue to the hot tip of the burning incense.

You can make a simple incense holder by taking a small piece of wood, clay, or a votive metal tin as an impromptu censer. If using wood, drill a hole in it for holding a stick incense. If you have any clay on hand, use a small amount of it to roll it into a ball. Flatten the top part of the clay, and then insert the incense stick into the clay's flattened top. If using a votive metal tin as an incense holder, you can paint the holder, add glitter to its exterior, or you can fill it with different colored sand. You might have to refresh the sand from time to time; over the course of use, burnt ashes will mix with the sand, so periodic refreshment is necessary.

Chalice

Description, Uses, and Symbolism

The chalice is a goblet or a cup used in ritual workings. Chalices are made of pewter, silver, brass, ceramic, glass, cold cast resin, or alternative materials. The chalice is a vessel used for libation or for sharing an offering and/or giving an offering to the Divine. Some practitioners use non-alcoholic beverages and others use wine for libation. The chalice is a symbol of the Divine Feminine: The unification of the stem and cup is representative of the God and Goddess or the masculine and feminine principles. As mentioned earlier, when you insert the athame, a phallic symbol, inside the opening of the cup, this serves as a symbolic representation of the unification of the God and Goddess or the creative nature of the Universe. The cup portion of the chalice symbolically represents the womb of the Goddess.

Making it Magickal

When placing the chalice on the altar, position it in the West, the cardinal direction associated with the element of water and the Divine feminine. Cleanse, bless, consecrate, and charge the chalice before use.

Care, Maintenance, and Cautions

If the chalice is made of glass, be very careful when handling or storing it. If you choose to make your chalice out of ceramics, you will have to make sure you glaze the cup correctly to prevent illness. In addition, if you are working with other Magickal practitioners, sometimes you might pass the libation cup from one practitioner to another in circle. You might want to forego this practice, especially if one or more practitioners is ill or has a weakened immune system. In such cases, it is perfectly acceptable to use separate cups for the purposes of libation. You can even invest in chalice sets containing as many as six or more different vessels for use in ritual.

For the Crafty Witch

If you are on a budget, try using a plain wine glass purchased at a flea market, garage sale, or dollar store for a chalice. Decorate the glass by adding crystals, dyed agate beads, shell beads, flat-back rhinestones, metal filigree jewelry pieces, or crystal stickers to the glass's exterior. You can also paint symbols on it with non-toxic paints. If adding something like crystal stickers to the exterior of the cup, reinforce the adhesive by using white epoxy or add a touch of glue to the backside of each sticker. If you have a small pentacle, you can use a glue gun to add the pentacle to the side of the glass. Make sure any embellishments you add to the glass do not hinder your ability to physically cleanse or drink from the vessel.

Offering Bowl

Description, Uses, and Symbolism

An offering bowl is a vessel you can use for placing offerings consisting of herbs, minerals, food, libation, or items collected from the natural world. You will use an offering bowl to express gratitude to the Divine or to appeal to the Divine for blessings.

An offering bowl should be a reasonable size, but also small enough to fit on your altar. The bowl can be any shape you desire, and it can be made of any material, although silver bowls are great for this purpose. The ideal offering bowl is made of materials that are representative of earth like glass, stone, ceramic, or wood. Do not use a plastic dish for an offering bowl since plastic is a synthetic material.

As a practitioner of the Magickal arts, it is important that you remain respectful of the Divine. You need to continue to recognize that you are playing a small role in the larger tapestry of the universe. Offerings allow you to express gratitude. The offering bowl contains the "symbolic sacrifice." If you leave food or other objects in the bowl, you are giving the Divine the quintessence or core spiritual qualities of the items you offer. The bowl is a symbol of giving, sharing, and gratitude.

Making it Magickal

The bowl you choose should be attractive. You will have to cleanse, bless, and consecrate it before use. Place the bowl in the North on the altar since the bowl is representative of the Earth. Carefully choose the items you place in the bowl: the best objects are natural and include things like flowers, herbs, incense, leaves, acorns, stones, or food.

Care, Maintenance, and Cautions

Never use the bowl for mundane applications. Periodically, you will have to empty and clean the bowl: this is particularly true if you put food products in it. If you use a silver offering bowl, use an appropriate metal cleaner to keep the bowl looking its best.

When placing food products in an offering bowl it is best if they are dry and that you avoid liquid offerings. You can make offerings of wet foods or beverages outdoors in an area where you do not have to worry about making a mess with the liquids. If you have a glass offering bowl, take care how you move the bowl around; make sure you always have a firm grip on the bowl when you move it.

For the Crafty Witch

Use a small ceramic container, a raised bowl, a glass jar, a pedestal bowl, a large abalone shell, a stainless steel bowl, or bowls made of copper, white metal, brass, soapstone, agate, green onyx, pewter, cobalt glass, red mosaic glass, or other materials. You can put your offerings outside in an area that you specifically dedicate as an offering area, but be cautious with outdoor offerings since food might attract wild animals to the offering area.

You can make a plain bowl more decorative for use as an offering bowl; use a glue gun or epoxy to attach mosaic tiles, feathers, stones, shells, and alternative items to the exterior of the bowl. If you have a pedestal bowl, embellish the dish's pedestal with leather, suede, feathers, ribbons, or your choice of décor. You can make your own bowl out of ceramic molds if you are so inclined. Alternatively, a clay pot will suffice as an offering bowl, and the porous clay material is easy to paint with your choice of non-toxic acrylics. You can even make a bowl by hand if you enjoy making pottery. If you choose a bowl made of wood, you can burn symbols into the side of the bowl too.

Pentacle

Description, Uses, and Symbolism

The pentacle is an upright five-pointed star, sometimes called a pentagram, inside of an enclosed circle. All of the points of the pentagram are touching the inner edge of the circular enclosure. This symbol, with one point in the ascendant, is a pentacle. When inverted, with two points in the ascendant, it is an inverted pentagram and has an entirely different symbolic meaning than a pentacle or upright pentagram.

A pentacle for Magickal workings can be made of clay, metal, wood, or alternative materials. Many practitioners wear the pentacle as an amulet (pronounced *am-u-lit*), and/or put it in the center of the altar for use during Magickal practices. When worn for the purposes of protection, the pentacle serves to ward off negative as well as to draw positive energies.

The pentacle is a symbol of the four cardinal directions and the spirit. The circular enclosure represents the never-ending cycle of life, death, and rebirth. The points for the pentacle represent Air, Fire, Earth, Water, and Akasha. All of the lines in the star of the pentacle create a single, continuous shape, while the circle has no beginning or ending point. The star inside the circle touches the circle at every point; thus, the pentacle connotes the eternal, everlasting, and the infinite. The pentacle is the symbol for The Void and the realm of Magick as well.

Making it Magickal

Cleanse, bless, consecrate, and charge the pentacle you buy or make before use.

Care, Maintenance, and Cautions

If you wear the pentacle every day as a symbol of protection, you may want to cleanse and re-consecrate the tool regularly, especially after encountering negative people and/or energies. When not in use, wrap the pentacle in a black cloth to protect it from undesirable energies as well. If you buy an inverted pentagram to use as an amulet, remember that even though the inverted pentagram has some positive symbols associated with it, the symbol also has negative connotations. Whether you wear a pentacle or a pentagram in public, it is very likely you will encounter one or more people that will misinterpret the meaning of the amulet. For more information about the significant differences between an upright pentacle and an inverted pentagram, see our book: *Wicca: What's the Real Deal? Breaking Through the Misconceptions* (Schiffer Publishing, 2011).

If your pentacle suddenly breaks or disappears without explanation, it can mean either one of two things: The pentacle has done its job protecting you and it is no longer intended for you, or the pentacle has absorbed significant negative energies and has fallen or broken free from its chain. If the pentacle turns black and becomes impossible to clean, it means the amulet/talisman has been heavily exposed to nasty energies and it is time to dispose of it by burying it. In both of the latter cases, it is time for you to look for a new pentacle.

For the Crafty Witch

If you do not have the money to buy a pentacle for Magickal workings, you can make one out of clay, pipe cleaners, or you can burn a pentacle onto a small, flat piece of wood. You can also choose a flat stone and paint a pentacle on it. If you happen to have a spare pentacle in your jewelry box, you can use it in Magickal workings.

You can make a beautiful pentacle out of mosaic tiles. Alternatively, you can use a cork coaster and paint a pentacle inside of it, or you can use beads and glue each bead onto the coaster to form a homemade pentacle. You can make a pentacle out of copper wire; you can carve one in candle wax or you can glue Popsicle sticks in the shape of a star onto a piece of round wood; paint or stain the wooden piece to give it some nice color.

Sea Salt

Description, Uses, and Symbolism

Sea Salt is a mineral created when sea or ocean water evaporates; it is sold in granulated form or as rock salt. The term *salt* comes from the Latin word *sal*, meaning the sea as well as wit or mental acuity.[17] Salt has long been considered holy and Magickal; writers like Homer referred to salt as being divine, and philosophers like Plato called the mineral something that should be viewed as "most sacred;" in fact, due to its preserving nature, in many cultures and religious systems salt symbolizes life.[18] Ancient Egyptians believed that salt, when consumed, could incite lust and forbad their priests from consuming it.[19] Some people from ancient cultures have used salt in exorcisms, to drive away evil forces, as a defense against the evil eye, as burnt offerings for deities, and a number of ancient cultures associated salt with the Sun and light.[20] Sea Salt is a purifier; for mundane purposes, it is used in the culinary arts, but for Magickal applications, it serves as a Magickal and medicinal tool.

Many cultures associate salt with cleansing and purification. Salt is representative of the Earth via its connection with the Divine Mother, and is therefore associated with the element of the North. Salt is a drying agent and it considered a mineral that purifies, protects, and cleanses people, places, and things of negative energies. Sometimes practitioners use salt to create a Magick circle, but you can also use it for the purposes of consecration or in all spells or rituals involving purification, protection, and healing. Sea Salt has a stronger taste than table salt. Since the sea is symbolic of the Divine Feminine, symbolically the mineral comes from the womb of the Goddess.

The understanding of salt as having protective or sacred properties has a long and rich history. Even in Christian beliefs, salt is associated with sacred properties. The ancient superstition or practice of throwing salt over one's left shoulder illustrates the way people have viewed the properties of salt. Whenever salt was spilt, casting it over the left shoulder was believed to ward off the devil, some pending evil, or a potential quarrel. Salt, especially in ancient times, was considered a valuable product, and to spill it foretold of something negative to come, that is, unless the individual responded appropriately to prevent the negative event from occurring.

The reason for casting salt over the left shoulder and not the right is that the left hand side has long been associated with all things sinister. Meanwhile, throwing spilt salt over the left shoulder may stem from biblical references. In the Bible, Lot's unnamed wife looks back on what was happening to Sodom and Gomorrah while it is destroyed. She is punished for doing so by being turned into a pillar of salt.[21] The story is a warning of not listening to the instruction of God, but it also holds the moral that you should not waste your time looking into the unchangeable past. Salt is a preservative, and Lot's wife, due to her own unfortunate curiosity, looked back upon Sodom and Gomorrah, and in doing so put herself in a position where she would remember or *preserve* the final moments of Sodom and Gomorrah in her mind. The act of throwing salt over one's shoulder to ward off evil might be linked to this depiction in the bible; the superstition also subtly hints that one should recall the fate of Lot's wife when looking upon the past longingly or for any length of time. Interestingly, in some cultures, people have used salt for the purposes of divination; for example, the ancient Chinese would burn salt and read the ashes to foretell the future. If we consider this notion of using salt to foretell future events, it makes the punishment of Lot's wife even more remarkable; her eternal form of punishment for looking back was being transformed into mineral used, by at least some cultures, for the purposes of divination or foretelling the future.

Making it Magickal

You should consecrate Sea Salt before using it; this helps to separate the salt's energies from those intended for mundane purposes. You can mix Sea Salt with water and consecrate it to create consecrated salt water.

Care, Maintenance, and Cautions

Sea Salt needs to be stored in a dry place so that moisture and humidity do not damage the consistency of the product. You will also want to store it away where renegade cooks in the home cannot inadvertently steal your supply! If you store Sea Salt on your altar in a bowl, you may want a small bowl with a lid so that the salt remains dry and free of dust.

Make sure that when you are working with Sea Salt that you do not get any in your eyes or in open cuts: the salt will irritate the skin and eyes. If you consume consecrated salt water for the purposes of bodily purification, do so only in small amounts: too much Sea Salt, even when diluted in water, can make you nauseous.

For the Crafty Witch

Sea Salt is preferred in Magickal applications, but if you do not have any, you can use consecrated table salt instead. Both forms of salt are easily accessible at your local grocery or dollar store and are about the same price. If you want to be creative about how you store your sea salt, you can make a decorative container for storing it.

***Note:** *Some practitioners place a bowl of Earth on their altar in addition to or instead of a bowl of salt. While it is perfectly acceptable to use Earth on the altar to represent the element, you will still require Sea Salt when you are making consecrated water or when you require salt in spell workings.*

The Wand and Staff

Description, Uses, and Symbolism

The wand and staff are air tools used to focus and send Magickal energies in a specific direction. The term wand comes from the Gothic word *wandu-s*, the Germanic word *wandu-z*, and the Swedish term *vand*, and etymologically suggests that the physical nature of the wand is sometimes flexible, supple, pliable, or agile,[22] particularly if the wand is made of wood. Some more contemporary Magickal wands are made of glass, bone, or hard metals, so the physical nature of the wand becomes less pliant. Nevertheless, the characteristics of pliancy, flexibility, and agility also connote the movement of the practitioner's will through the wand during Magickal workings; the Magick wand or staff serves as an extension of the practitioner and is used to direct one's inner energies, will, and intentions outwardly so that they can produce results in the physical realm.

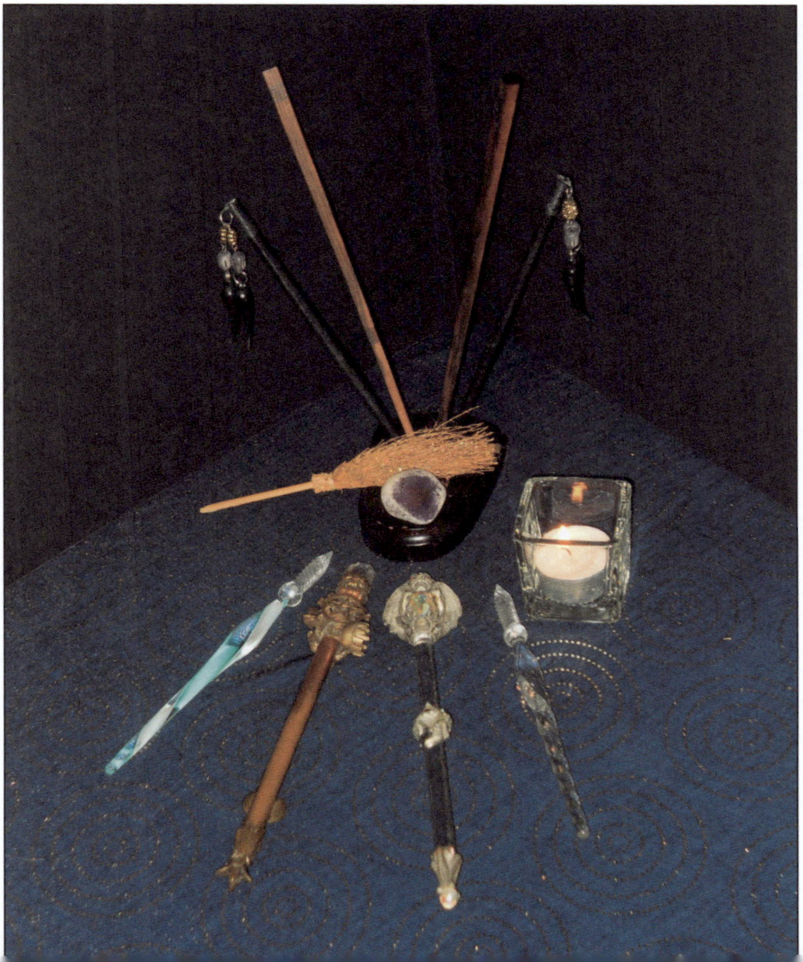

A wand or staff is made of a variety of woods including African Blackwood, Apple, Ash, Bacote, Beach, Birch, Black Walnut, Blackthorn, Bloodwood, Canarywood, Chestnut, Hawthorn, Hazel, Holly, Juniper, Kingwood, Mahogany, Miniosa, Oak, Olivewood, Redwood, Rosewood, Rowan, Teak, Tulipwood, Wayfaring, Wenge, Wild Cherry, Wild Honeysuckle, Willow, Wych Elm, Yew, and other woods. Wands are also made of hematite, quartz crystal, rose quartz, amethyst, ruby zoisite, bloodstone, carnelian, moonstone, kyanite, selenite, black onyx, copper, fired clay, pewter, glass, bone, deer antler, or a mixture of materials. Wands vary in size and can range from three to twenty inches or more, depending on the practitioner's preference. Staffs are far larger, and, in terms of measurement, are usually, but not necessarily, taller than the user. The materials used in creating the wand can augment the energies passed through the tool during Magickal workings.

Wands and staffs have long been associated with miracles, Magick, the movement or direction of personal will, and Divine power. Wands were used as Magickal tools in pre-dynastic Egypt; the ancient Egyptians believed that the soul, or "ka," separated from the body at death, but that the ka endured as long as the physical body remained intact. Believing that the ka still required food and sustenance, Egyptians would leave items for the deceased so that their needs were satisfied in the afterlife, and things like weapons, food, personal items, Magickal texts, and a Magick wand were left in or nearby the tomb so that the tools and items proved accessible to the soul.[23] Ancient Druids carried a wand or consecrated staff; doing so was indicative of their initiation into the mysteries.[24] In the Roman catacombs, Christian artists depict Jesus Christ raising Lazarus while holding a wand to perform the miracle of resurrection.[25] Since the ancient Hebrews attributed Magick and sacred powers to wands or rods, this image likens Christ to Moses, who also wielded a divine rod or staff.[26] The latter assertion rings particularly true with practitioners who view Christ, not as the son of God, but as a healer and magician.

The wand or staff is associated with the cardinal direction of East and the element of Air. Since the wand is phallic-like in appearance, it symbolizes fertility as well as the masculine aspect of the Divine. The wand also symbolizes the movement of energy as you project your inner intent into the mundane world; with a wand, you penetrate the boundaries of the inner world and project your energies into the outer world for the purposes of direction and manifestation. The wand serves as a symbolic extension of the practitioner. It represents air, and the speed of movement absent of physical restraints. Some practitioners associate the wand with the element of fire as well, since it is a tool used to extend one's will and to project it into the mundane plane. You can use a wand/staff in spell casting, circle casting, and ritual workings.

Making it Magickal

Cleanse, bless, consecrate, and charge your wand/staff before use. If it is made of wood, you can carve runes into it or paint Magickal symbols on it. For example, you might want to add your Magickal name on your wand or staff written in runes. Some Witches choose to name all of their tools, and if you do so, you can carve the name of your tool in rune onto the surface.

Care, Maintenance, and Cautions

Keep your tool free of dust and debris. Like the altar, you should re-consecrate the wand/staff whenever you feel it necessary to do so. When not in use, wrap the wand in black cloth or place it inside a black bag to keep the item protected from stagnated or negative energies. You can also store it in an appropriate size box.

When you are using the wand/staff, consider your surroundings; do not wave the wand too closely to lit incense or candles. Since the wand can have a pointed end, especially if it has crystals added, you will want to make sure that children, animals, or other practitioners are not nearby as you wield it. If you are participating in a coven working and you are using the wand/staff to cast circle, make sure that any other members are free and clear from the end of your wand/staff when it is in use.

For the Crafty Witch

When money is tight and you cannot afford to buy a wand/staff, you can make your own out of a stick of wood. You can also use a substitute tool like a spear in place of a staff if you desire. In fact, some practitioners prefer handmade tools to store-bought tools; by making your own Magickal tool, you are imbuing the tool with your Magickal energies. You can also make a wand by using a hair stick, a thin paintbrush, a wooden dowel, chopsticks, or even a calligraphy pen. When all else fails, you can simply use your finger to direct Magickal energies.

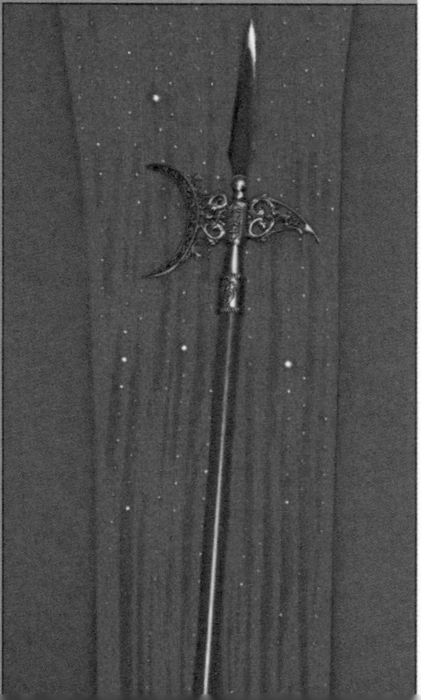

If you choose to make your wand/staff from a stick of wood, try to find a stick that is as straight as possible. You can use a knife to peel off the bark in order to expose the smooth wood underneath. You can use a razor knife to cut off the small wooden nubs that protrude from the stick if any are present. Sand down the stick of wood, paying particular attention to the areas where you removed any protruding pieces of wood, paint or stain it, and adorn it with small crystals or stones. You can also wrap the surface of the wand/staff with copper wire, ribbon, suede, leather, or some other kind of fabric material to add additional decorative elements.

Water

Description, Uses, and Symbolism

Nearly three quarters of the planet Earth is covered in water, and all life forms need water for survival. Water serves as the symbolic representation of the Divine feminine, since all living things and their survival is dependent on the element. Water is the life-blood of the Earth Mother, and it has many uses in ritual workings. In *Cosmic Energy: How to Harness the Invisible Power Around You to Transform Your Life*, author Anne Jirsch asserts the power of water and its ability to be transformed by intent; citing the work of Dr. Masaru Emoto, Jirsch explains that when water is exposed to certain thought forms, intentions, or music, that the physical properties of water crystals change. In fact, the properties of the water crystals are influenced by positive and negative energies; when the intention, thought form or music is positive or beautiful, the water crystal formation is also beautiful. If the water is exposed to negative thoughts, intention, or music, than the crystals become malformed or distorted.[27] Thus, as you bless, charge, and consecrate water, even if it is water from the tap, you are not only spiritually preparing the water, you are physically changing its properties as well.

Making it Magickal

Keep a small bowl or vessel of consecrated salt water on your altar. Bless and consecrate the water before you use it if you're transforming the water into holy water; if however, you are using the water for spell workings, bless, consecrate, and charge the water so you can successfully alter the water's properties in a way that aligns the water with the intent of your Magickal working. When you place your consecrated water on the altar, place it in the West, since this is the cardinal direction associated with the water element.

Care, Maintenance, and Cautions

Refresh the container of water on your altar weekly so that the water does not become stagnant. You will need to bless and consecrate the water every time you refresh it. You should keep the water in an enclosed container to prevent accidental spills.

For the Crafty Witch

Fresh spring water is ideal for use in Magickal applications. You can also use tap water if need be. The container you use for consecrated water can be an old wine bottle, a decorative wine decanter, an amber, clear, or cobalt blue glass bottle, a French square glass bottle, a large vial, a corked bottle, a swing top bottle, or a jug. If you are looking to align the bottle with the element of water, clear or blue bottles work best. If you plan to take consecrated salt water with you when you travel, a small plastic bottle will do. For sabbats or other special occasions, add a touch of colored drink mix to the water to give it a color that matches the color theme of the sabbat or event.

Chapter 2
Other Essential Tools

"Magic, like technology, is a tool."
—Mercedes Lackey

Tools for Magickal Record Keeping

It is important to keep track of your Magickal experiences and practices for a number of reasons. First, in tracking your Magickal experiences you can start to identify things or situations that trigger your psychic abilities. You can also use journaling to record spell success so that you can improve your spell casting abilities over the course of time. Meanwhile, tracking Magickal experiences helps you reflect on the self; you can assess your journal entries to examine how your spiritual growth progresses. Magickal record keeping is also important when you want to keep track of your favorite spells and rituals, all of which you can store in your personal grimoire.

Book of Shadows

Description, Uses, and Symbolism

A Book of Shadows, also sometimes called a *grimoire,* is a Witch's collection of spells, rituals, and miscellaneous Magickal knowledge. A Book of Shadows is no ordinary journal and ideally, you should keep it as a separate *grimoire,* even aside from Tarot, dream, and psychic journals. It serves as a personal anthology of Magickal studies and workings. It is your portfolio of Magickal applications, occult development, and Magickal experiences. Keep your book private and safe from prying eyes. This book is a compilation of spells, rituals, healing experiences, and it is a text that grows as your knowledge increases. You may even end up with more than one Book of Shadows over the course of time.

Making it Magickal

You can get a book with a locking device if it makes you feel more secure. Some Witches choose to write their entire Book of Shadows in runes, an ancient type of alphabet; this allows practitioners the chance to simultaneously encrypt and empower the material they are documenting. Some also choose to write their materials in red ink; red being the color of blood and the life force, serves to empower the words written. When writing in red and in rune, the words documented are therefore doubly empowered; the words are etched with red ink so they are formed with the energies or vibrational influences of the color red, and when writing in rune, you have concentrated on each letter as you convert the written words into the coded, runic alphabet you choose. Bless the book and bind it to you before you begin using it; you can use one of the following blessing/binding spells to keep your book protected.

Book Binding and Blessing 1

This spell is for binding a book to you so that no one takes it from you without your consent, or if you loan the book to another individual, the borrower will return it. You can use the spell on any book you desire, but it is especially useful for protecting your *grimoires*, Magickal experimentation notes, and your Magickal journals.

Hold the book in your receptive hand while positioning your projective hand over the front of the book you want to bind. Visualize a bright blue, fiery cord forming in the palm of your hand and wrapping around the exterior of the book. Watch the cord as it fastens itself into a tight knot: one impossible to untie. Say the following:

> I call upon the Guardians of the East, North, South, and West,
> Through your powers, this book be blessed.
> I call upon the Wards of the West, South, North, and East,
> Upon this hour, your protection I beseech.
> Wind Guardian and the whispering secrets you keep,
> Earth Guardian, whose eyes know not of dream or sleep,
> Fire Guardian, keeper of the jubilant flame in endless dance,
> Water Guardian, keeper of clandestine oceans, infinite and vast,

I call upon the Ancient Guardians Four,
This book to safe keep I implore.
This tome, its pages, no unworthy eye shall see,
Borrowed or loaned, by this binding, returns back unto me.
So mote it be. Blessed be.

Book Binding and Blessing 2

Hold the book you are binding/blessing in your receptive hand. Place your projective hand on top of the book and say:

I bless this book by powers that be,
To keep it safe from sea to sea,
That it will always return to me,
No matter where I may be,
To keep it safe and keep it sound,
Always able to be found,
When I call you to come home,
No longer will you have to roam,
You are blessed, but are not free,
When desired, come home to me!
As I will, so mote it be!

Care, Maintenance, and Cautions

Since this is a book storing your Magickal recipes, spells, rites, and secrets, you will want to keep your Book of Shadows in a place where it remains safe from prying eyes. Take steps to ensure that you do not expose the Book of Shadows to too much sunlight, humidity, or water, all of which can destroy the pages within your *grimoire*.

For the Crafty Witch

Head to your local bookstore and get a book with lined or unlined blank pages to create your own Book of Shadows. You can also use a notebook, a journal, or a diary to begin your Book of Shadows, but eventually you will find that you want something more elaborate or special.

If you want to include artwork, sketches, and drawings in your Book of Shadows, you will be better off with unlined blank pages. If you want to maintain a straight edge for writing out spells and rituals, you can use a ruler to lightly map out the guidelines you need to keep everything neat. Once you have documented the ritual or spell, you can gently erase the guidelines you have used on the blank page. Make sure you do not press down on the pencil too hard; otherwise, the guidelines will be very difficult to get rid of later.

You can also make a Book of Shadows out of a binder and loose-leaf paper; this type of record keeping allows for the easy rearrangement of your materials later on, too. If you want to keep the pages protected, you can get plastic page protectors for little expense. If you want to make the exterior of the binder or blank book attractive, add decorative components, letters, gems, stickers, and whatever else appeals to you.

Book of Mirrors

Description, Uses, and Symbolism

A Book of Mirrors is a notebook, journal, or blank book where you record your day-to-day Magickal experiences. A Book of Mirrors is a useful tool for the neophyte and adept practitioner alike; for a new practitioner, this journal will help you discover when your power days are, how you receive different psychic messages, and it will allow you to monitor your development as a practitioner. For the adept practitioner, the Book of Mirrors proves a useful tracking tool: one that helps identify distinct patterns, synchronicities, and the appearance of repetitious messages from the universe. This book is a Magickal diary where you will document all of your daily experiences; as you add notations in this book pay careful attention to the date, the weather, the moon phase, the environment, your location, who accompanied you, and your mood. A Book of Mirrors reflects your Magickal experiences back to you on a daily basis; it stands as a continued reflection of insights, messages, synchronicities, and it helps you develop a connection to the God, Goddess, animal totems, nature, and the Universe, as well as your own intuition.

Making it Magickal

Cleanse, bless, consecrate, and bind your Book of Mirrors. If you get a blank book, you can decorate it with occult symbols or you can even glue a small, decorative mirror to the front of the book. Smudge the book periodically to keep it free of negative energies.

Care, Maintenance, and Cautions

Use the same care that you use for your Book of Shadows for your Book of Mirrors. You will want to keep it in a safe area, out of sunlight and away from any sources of water.

For the Crafty Witch

Carry a digital recorder with you and vocally record your experiences until you get a chance to jot them down later on; this will save you from having to have your Book of Mirrors on hand wherever you are.

Divination Journal

Description, Uses, and Symbolism

There is more to performing divination than choosing a tool that appeals to you. The process of journaling is just as important as the act of practicing divination on a regular basis. Since any information obtained during divinatory practices does not come from the tool itself, but from the universe, you are engaging in communication with the Divine. Therefore, you should make clear notes about the messages you receive. As you interact with the Universe, your own knowledge of symbols will influence your ability to understand intuitive messages. Journaling will allow you to see your successes and oversights during divinatory sessions. As you journal your divinatory experiences, you will want to be honest in your recordings; documenting "hits" and "misses" as they occur helps you grow as well as improve your divinatory methods.

There is much to gain by documenting errors and speculations as well. If you document what went wrong, unverifiable experiences, and things divined incorrectly, you can learn from past mistakes and become a better diviner because of it. Through documenting speculations and errors, you might identify factors that are hindering your practice, like emotional issues, anxiety/stress, or confusing emotional desires with actual intuitive messages.

It may prove helpful to use different colored ink during the documentation process. Use black ink to document the reading, divinatory message, or psychic experience; a blue pen for documenting your emotions/hope/fears before, during, and after the experience; a green pen for documenting identified themes, colors, repetitious events, or symbols identified; and a red pen to document any verification you receive or the actual outcome. Ultimately, this journal is not just a place for logging your psychic/divinatory experiences; it is a living process and one that develops with you through the course of your practices.

Making it Magickal

Cleanse, bless, and bind the journal before using it. You can also smudge it periodically with sage to keep it free of negative energies.

Care, Maintenance, and Cautions

Avoid conducting and documenting your divinatory experience if you are in a negative mood. This can leave negative energies attached to the book and it can hinder your ability to assess your experiences before you document them. Eventually, you will have to replace your divinatory journal with a new one; give the new journal the same initial treatment as you did with the first by cleansing, blessing, binding, and consecrating it.

For the Crafty Witch

You can choose any kind of journal for psychic journaling, but you will need to reserve the journal for documenting divinatory and psychic experiences alone. If you choose a large notebook with multiple sections or if you use a binder with loose-leaf paper, create separate sections based on the type of divination you are performing or the kinds of psychic experiences you are having. You can make sections for Tarot, runes, crystal gazing, intuitive experiences, synchronistic experiences, and the like. You also have the option of keeping a chronological journal. If you divide your journal into different psychic/divinatory experiences, make sure you date and time stamp each recording for easier tracking. As you record each experience, leave enough room for adding more materials later on; you may find that you want to document anything that happens that serves as verification for your psychic/divinatory experiences.

Colored Inks, Parchment, and Magickal Alphabets

Magickal practitioners understand that every color vibrates with a specific energy, so inks of every color can add different energies to what you write. Here is a brief guide of the energies that each color carries whenever you use it in Magickal applications:*

Red: This is a power color because it is the color of the life force or blood. When you write in red ink, you are charging your Magickal workings, journals, and Book of Shadows with powerful energies.

Orange: Orange is a color you need to be careful when using; this color is not only indicative of autumnal themes or energies associated with success, but it also is an attractant. If you are not careful about what you write in orange, you could end up attracting undesirable energies.

Yellow: For a spell pertaining to communication, new beginnings, or inspiration, you can use yellow ink to write the spell; using yellow ink will align your writings with your desired result.

Green: This is the color representative of the earth and is therefore a grounding color. If you are conducting spell working where you are trying to reclaim balance in a situation or to regain emotional balance, green is a good color to use. Green is also associated with the material plane so it corresponds with fertility, abundance, money, and earthly gains.

Blue: Blue is associated with the element of water; it is a good ink to use in Magickal applications involving psychic healing, the subconscious, and spells dealing with emotional concerns or issues.

Indigo and Violet: Purple is associated with Akasha, the fifth element, and the combination of all the elements. This color has the highest vibration out of all of the other colors. Purple is associated with royalty, and it is a good color for use in all spell workings.

*For a more in-depth explanation of colors and their Magickal properties, see Chapter 5.

Magickal Alphabets and Parchment

You can use parchment for documenting and performing spells, but parchment is not an essential for Magickal workings: any kind of paper will work. Parchment tends to be more expensive than regular paper too. Some practitioners prefer to use parchment because doing so helps to lend to the seriousness of the work.

Magickal alphabets or runes are ancient and powerful images that are associated with letters of the alphabet and/or specific meanings. The term *rune* in Middle English had the same spelling and means counsel; the word is further derived from the Anglo-Saxon *rún,* meaning "*whisper*" or "*secret conference.*"[1] The idea of runes being secret has a two-fold meaning. First, since runes are some of the oldest alphabets ever used by various cultures around the world, they were known to a select few, so their use was considered privileged knowledge or a secret. Additionally, you can use runes in divinatory practices as a "secret conference" with Divine forces; the outcome of rune casting is understood as a form of "mysterious and whispering communication" from the cosmos. You can find out more about runes and divination in Chapter 4.

There are many runes to use to write in your Magickal texts. You can even create your own when you become skilled enough at using them. If you use runes to write your spells, it forces you to focus or concentrate when you are writing. Through greater concentration, you further empower the spell with your intent. Some of the runes you can choose from include Anglo-Saxon Futhorc, Angelic, Celestial Script, Danish Futhark, Elder Futhark, Enochian, Malachim, Medieval Futhark, Norwegian Futhark, Phoenician, Pictish Script, or Theban. You can find Magickal rune fonts online too, if you want to use runes in your word processing applications. You should choose a rune that you find visually appealing or that you find meaningful to you. It can take some practice getting used to writing in rune and converting words into runic letters, but the more you use runes, the easier the process becomes.

Amulets and Talismans

Description, Uses, and Symbolism

An amulet is a charged item that you can wear for the purposes of protection. Amulets defend against baneful conditions, malevolent energies, and evil forces; ironically, amulets were formerly worn as a defense against witchcraft. The term *amulet* is rooted in the French word *amulette* and the Italian word *amuleto*.[2] Some sources suggest that the term *amulet* is rooted in the Latin word *amulētum,* a word derived from Arabic term *hamalât* meaning *"to carry, bear, or to wear,"* but the etymological connection is dubious at best.[3] Sometimes an amulet is identified as a charm or preservative due to its protective nature. Other times, people wear amulets because they believe the amulet provides them with luck.

The term talisman (pronounced *tal-is-man*) is derived from the Arabic word *tilsamân* meaning "a charm," and the Greek term *télesma* meaning "mystery."[4] It is interesting to note that the terms *amulet* and *talisman* are often interchanged, but there are subtle differences between the two objects. First, while a talisman can serve the same purposes as an amulet, the user does not always carry the talisman. Further, some sources ascribe more power to the talisman than the amulet, suggesting that the amulet is a defensive charm, thus serving as a barrier against negativity, while a talisman is more effective or powerful than an amulet, having the ability to render extensive influence at great distances.[5] Amulets and talisman are used for spiritual protection, but they are also worn/carried to give the wearer peace of mind.

The belief that an amulet or talisman has protective powers is vital if you expect the objects to work; doubt in the properties of the amulet or talisman and its ability to offer protection will render the items ineffective. Amulets and talismans can sometimes serve as a symbol of one's faith, beliefs, or predilections as well. For instance, some Witches wear a pentacle as a form of protection, but the symbol also serves as an emblem of the wearer's faith. Alternatively, you may have an affinity for Egyptian jewelry; you can wear an ankh, the symbol of eternal life and resurrection, as an amulet or you can carry one with you as a talisman.

The Babylonians, Egyptians, Grecians, Romans, Chinese, Japanese, and myriad other cultures have used amulets for protection from disease, ailments, accidents, illnesses, and baneful energies or situations. For example, the Ancient Egyptians often wore amulets that were effigies or miniaturized depictions of one or more deities in the Egyptian pantheon. The living carried amulets to ensure prosperity, luck, protection, and the favor of the Gods and Goddesses, but amulets were also buried with the deceased so that the dead could remain protected and favored in the afterlife. When the ancient Egyptians mummified the dead, they would often place amulets inside the mummy wrappings,[6] otherwise known as the Tresses of Nephthys (*pronounced Nef-thus*).

Not all amulets are made of gemstones, stones, or precious metals. For instance, medicine bags, a small bag containing a variety of herbs and/or stones used for protection and/or healing, can serve as amulets. Some of the earliest amulets and talismans were nothing more than specific words or names of deities written onto parchment. The parchment would then be placed in a small receptacle and worn by the carrier in a ring or suspended from the neck.

Birthstones, when included in a piece of jewelry, are a type of amulet,[7] and if carried on the person, they are a talisman. There are twelve signs of the zodiac, each associated with a different stone. These stones are often worn, not only for their attractiveness, but also for the element of luck they provide to the wearer. In fact, some birthstones are believed to be appropriate only for the person born within the specific month that the stone represents. This is especially true in the case of the opal, a stone associated with the month of October. Superstition holds that if you buy an opal for yourself or you wear it and you are not born in October, you will bring bad luck into your life. According to this lore, the only time a person that is not born in the month of October can wear an opal is if the stone or jewelry piece was given to the individual as a gift.

Making it Magickal

If you make your own amulets and talismans, they are empowered with personal energies, will, and intent. If you purchase amulets or talisman, you need to cleanse, bless, consecrate, and charge them before use. Add your own personal touches to the amulets and talismans you buy, thereby lending more of your own personal energies to them.

Care, Maintenance, and Cautions

The method of caring for an amulet or talisman in a physical sense is totally dependent on the materials used to make the tool. In a spiritual sense, cleanse or smudge the item as necessary. If you are wearing an amulet and the chain breaks, cleanse the amulet and replace the chain. When an amulet tarnishes or changes color and you can clean it, the item can still be used, provided you cleanse it before wearing it. If, however, the amulet or talisman turns a different color and is no longer cleanable, you will have to dispose of it by burying it.

For the Crafty Witch

If you like making jewelry, make your own amulets and charge them with your specific intentions. If you like drawing you can create amulets on parchment and decorate them with esoteric symbols of protection; then put the pieces of parchment in a small container or receptacle to wear them. Alternatively, you can carry parchment with words, verses, and/or symbols as a talisman. You can make a small mixture of herbs and carry it in a bag in your pocket or on your waist, or you can also create an amulet by adding herbs to a small receptacle and suspending it from a chain.

Besom

Description, Uses, and Symbolism

A besom (pronounced *bee-zum* or *bez-zum*) is a term used to describe the Witch's broom. Witches were at one time called besom-riders; this was based on the erroneous idea that witches rode on brooms as they flew through the sky. The term *besom* is rooted in the German word *bezem* and the Dutch word *bezen*, both meaning broom.[8] The term besom also means to "sweep something away via assertive, aggressive, or violent action"[9]; this notion can apply to how the besom is used when one is sweeping out negative energies. In ancient times, the besom was a broom crafted out of twigs or other woody materials;[10] the twigs were tied together and attached to a wooden handle. Besoms are commonly used in home cleansings, clearings, fertility rites, and to establish sacred space by sweeping an area free of negative or malevolent energies.

The handle of the besom represents the masculine aspect and the bush-like twigs represent the feminine aspect; thus, like the chalice and the bell, the broom is symbolic of sexuality and of the Divine feminine and masculine. Since the besom is a fertility symbol, it is a common tool used in handfastings. The act of "jumping the broom" serves to bless the wedded couple with fertility. To step over the besom together as a couple serves as an omen that the couple will soon wed.

Making it Magickal

If you buy a broom or make one yourself and decide to use it as a besom, do not use the broom for mundane purposes. You should bless, charge, and consecrate the besom before using it. Carve symbols in the handle of the besom if you desire. Your besom should not have a plastic handle or a broom end made of nylon materials, since such materials are synthetic.

Care, Maintenance, and Cautions

Since your besom will have dried materials to form the broom portion of the tool, you should keep it away from any flames. When not used, keep it stored in a dry place, and do not use the broom for regular chores or housework.

For the Crafty Witch

You can make your own besom by finding a relatively straight stick or branch from a tree. You can remove the bark from the branch, and sand it down to remove any rough areas. You can use straw, birch, or any woody plant to create the end of the broom; you can bind the twigs to the branch with leather, suede, or durable twine. You can also use a fireplace broom as a besom, since many fireplace brooms have a metal handle. You can add decorative elements to your besom like ribbon, suede wrappings around the handle, or you can spray the broom portion with spray glitter. You can also paint the handle different colors, or add gemstones and other decorative embellishments to the handle of the broom.

Candle Snuffer

Description, Uses, and Symbolism

A candle snuffer looks like a small mallet-less bell with a long handle. The snuffer is made of stainless steel or silver, but you can also find candle snuffers made of copper or bronze as well. Like the besom, chalice, and the bell, a candle snuffer represents the unification of the masculine and feminine divine; the bell-like end of the snuffer represents the womb, and the phallic-like handle represents the masculine aspect of divinity. Candle snuffers are used for extinguishing flames, and are preferred by some practitioners who feel that it is insulting to the Gods to blow candles out or that to blow out candles when performing candle Magick is to blow the Magickal energies away from you instead of drawing positive results to you. The word *snuffer* comes from the German word *schnuppe*; the term *snuff* further refers to the "exhausted wick of a burning candle."[11] A snuffer cuts off the air supply to a flame and removes the "snuff" of the candlewick so that the flame goes out. While the use of a candle snuffer suppresses the flame physically, it does not suppress it on an astral level; thus, in rituals or spells, the flame continues to burn as well as to transmit one's intentions on the astral plane.

Making it Magickal

Cleanse, bless, and consecrate your candle snuffer. Once you have chosen a candle snuffer, use it only for snuffing out ritual candles or candles you use during meditation or spell work.

Care, Maintenance, and Cautions

When using a candle snuffer, take considerable care as you snuff out the flame; do not push the end of the snuffer too hard down onto the flame because you can end up breaking off the wick or you can end up burying the wick in wax. When you use the snuffer, if your first few attempts to snuff out the flame fail, allow the candle to burn a few more minutes before making another attempt. Do not touch the end of the candle snuffer immediately after snuffing out a candle; the inside of the snuffer may have hot wax on it and the metal transfers heat, so you can suffer from burns if you are not careful.

For the Crafty Witch

If you do not have a candle snuffer, use a small heat resistant glass to snuff out flames. You can use a metal engraver and engrave esoteric symbols on the snuffer. If you have some charms, you can hang them from the end of the snuffer's handle, or you can wrap the handle with suede, leather, or alternative materials.

Cauldron

Description, Uses, and Symbolism

The cauldron is a boiler or kettle; the pot can vary in size. The term *cauldron* comes from the French word *chaudron* as well as the Latin *caldus* meaning, "hot."[12] Cauldrons are cast iron, steel, or copper pots used for cooking in ancient times. Cauldrons come in an array of sizes; small, portable cauldrons are sometimes referred to as gypsy pots; at present, practitioners of Magick use them for mixing and burning herbs, scrying, making potions, and other Magickal purposes.

The cauldron is associated with the feminine divine; it stands as a symbol of transformation, change, fertility, and metamorphosis. The cauldron is sometimes associated with the cardinal direction of the North as well as the element of Earth; in some mythologies, the cauldron is a symbol of the secreted cave or a place where one accesses the underworld. The cauldron, also known as the Goddess's womb, is also a symbol of the subconscious mind and the secret mysteries. The cauldron's symbolic link to the subconscious and the underworld makes it a tool that is associated with the element of Water too. This tool is associated with the Fire Element since it is a tool that can be used to heat things, but also in a metaphorical sense, where it can represent the hot lava in the earth, set inside the protective rock casing of a naturally formed volcano.

As it is associated with the South, this tool becomes representative of the Mother Goddess, plenty, abundance, and nourishment of the spirit and body. Understood as the cauldron of knowledge or the deep well of the subconscious mind, the tool also becomes something associated with the element of Air, signifying wisdom, creativity, and communication. As the ideal Akashic tool, the cauldron represents the great abyss, the eternal void, the realm of Magick, and the very birthing of the universe.

The cauldron is sometimes used in spells and rituals for the purposes of burning spell components and breaking them down into ash, for mixing herbs or oils, for making potions, and for rites or spells specifically focused on fertility, abundance, the earth, or the spirit realm. You can use a cauldron as a divinatory tool by filling it with water and using it for scrying.

When burning something in the cauldron for the purposes of completing a spell, like parchment or paper, you can add powdered incense or herbs to the cauldron. If you only have stick incense, you can simply scrape a bit of the incense off the stick with your boline; the incense comes right off. Even if you only have cone incense, you can crush down the cone into a powder-like substance before you use it. For easier burning you can place the incense or herbs inside the parchment or paper and fold the paper up to keep the herbs/incense contained as it burns; you can light the paper and allow it to burn down to ashes inside the cauldron. Before removing the ashes and releasing them into the wind, allow the ashes to cool completely. If your cauldron is too large to carry outside, you can put the ashes into a small dish to take the cooled ashes outdoors later.

Making it Magickal

You should cleanse, bless, consecrate, and charge your cauldron. You can paint esoteric symbols on the exterior of the cauldron, or buy a cauldron that already has symbols on it. Smudge the cauldron periodically to keep it free from negative energies. When not in use, store the cauldron in an area where you perform ritual or other Magickal applications, thereby allowing the tool to accumulate the positive ritual or Magickal energies.

Care, Maintenance, and Cautions

When using a cauldron for liquids, you might find that the interior of the cauldron develops rust spots. Use ketchup on small spots to remove rust; the acidic nature of tomatoes can help in alleviating mild rust or corrosive conditions. You can use steel wool to work out the rust spots inside your cauldron; rinse the area you are cleaning periodically to see how much rust you have successfully removed. Bear in mind, however, scrubbing the cast iron in your cauldron with rough materials may lead to having to repaint the surface of the cauldron in the future.

Whenever you burn anything in the cauldron, use caution to avoid burning yourself, and that the area where the cauldron is situated is free of flammable or explosive materials. Additionally, if you burn anything inside the cauldron, leave ample time for the materials to cool down before disposing of the ash and residues.

For the Crafty Witch

If you cannot find a large cast iron pot, you can get a small tabletop cauldron online or at local specialty shops. It can be fun to search for old gypsy pots for sale online as well as at antique shops in your local area.

If you have a cauldron with a handle, you can decorate the handle with real or silk flowers, as long as you do not plan to burn anything in the cauldron; heat can cause real flowers to die off quickly and it can ruin silk flowers. If it is cast iron and you do not care for the black iron color, try painting it a different color; for instance, if you will be using it as a primary tool for scrying you might consider spray-painting it blue. If you plan to use the cauldron to heat things and you want to paint it, make sure you purchase high heat or heat resistant spray paint.

Cords

Description, Uses, and Symbolism

The term cord is rooted in the Latin word *chorda*, used to describe the strings made for stringed instruments, but since the word has evolved into cord, the term describes any type of string comprised of a variety of materials.[13] In Magickal applications, you can use cords for a variety of purposes. You can get them in the fabric section of your local craft or department store. When choosing a cord for use in Magick, you will want to consider your color selection; color plays an important role in the energies of the tools or items you use. For instance, if you decide to use a cord for binding the hands of two people being handfasted (wed), you would use a white cord about a foot long in length. The handfasting officiant (Priest or Priestess) then wraps the cord lightly around the wrists of the bride and groom; the binding cord symbolizes the union of the two souls in marriage.

You can use cords in cord Magick and for Magickal bindings. The Magickal symbolism of the cord is understood as something that is woven or twisted together with the ability to confine, bind, or restrict an object, item, or individual. Cords also Magickally symbolize the act of bringing something together or unification. You can use cords to take the measure of another practitioner. The act of taking the measure of a practitioner involves a rite that binds the practitioner to the words that they speak or to the oath that they take. You will need a cord that is the same length of the person's height. The cord represents the essence of the practitioner since there are a number of "cords" running through the human body including the spinal cord, the vocal cords, and ligaments. The cord can also be a symbolic representation of the silver cord that attaches the human soul to the physical body.

Making it Magickal

Cleanse, bless, consecrate, and charge any cords you use in any Magickal workings. For the use of a cord in a measure, you can choose a color that corresponds with a person's dominant element (white, red, blue, green, or purple): a factor determined by a person's characteristics, behaviors, and attributes. For instance, if a person is strong-willed, potentially stubborn, or well grounded, you can choose a green cord for representing the dominant earth element in their personality. Alternatively, if a person is highly empathic and emotive, you can choose a blue cord representing the dominant element of water. Someone with a fiery will and attitude can have a red measure cord, and yellow is ideal for someone who might be a good communicator or for someone who might be flighty. When all else fails, you can use a white cord for taking someone's measure since white can substitute any color or use a purple cord because purple represents Akasha, or the combination of all the elements. Once the measure is taken, you should secure the cord in a box and store it in a safe place.

Cords are also good for making a Witch's Ladder: a spell for healing, protection, or for deflecting negative energies. When making a Witch's Ladder, you should have a cord that is roughly three feet in length. You require a cord that is longer for this particular task since you will be tying a number of knots in the cord. After you choose your cord, bless and consecrate it. As you speak the spell to create the Witch's Ladder, you will need to say a line for every knot you create. Following the spell's completion, you have a cord that has knots running down the length from top to bottom.

Care, Maintenance, and Cautions

A few good rules to remember when binding anything include:

- Never bind yourself to another person unless both you and the individual in question freely choose to be bound to one another, such as the binding performed in a handfasting rite. It is unethical to bind yourself to another against that person's knowledge and free will.
- When binding an object, like a book or tool to you, wrap the cord toward you, not away from you; this keeps the energies of the object or tool connected to you.
- When binding someone from using Magick to harm, you should wrap the cord in a direction that is away from you, in order prevent that individual's energies or actions being bound to you.

For the Crafty Witch

If you do not have any thick cord available to you, you can cut six to nine pieces of yarn of equal length, and braid them together to make a cord. You can choose yarn of different colors to make a variety of cords for future use, or can use a drapery cord as a substitute.

Mortar and Pestle

Description, Uses, and Symbolism

The term *mortar* is derived from the Latin *mortarium*, the French *mortier*, and the Finnish *murta*, meaning, "to break." It also comes from the Dutch word *murlen* meaning, "to crush or mash."[14] The mortar is a small receptacle or bowl often made of glass, wood, stone, brass, marble, or soapstone. The interior of the bowl is cup shaped, and the tool is used for crushing and/or pounding herbs, small stones, and anything else you want to turn into a powdery substance. When you buy a mortar, it comes with a pestle; the term *pestle* is derived from the Latin term *pinsere* and the Sanskit *pis* meaning "to grind."[15] The pestle is a phallic or club shaped tool hosting a curved end used for crushing and pounding materials. Bear in mind that not all mortars are round, and can be square, bucket-shaped, cauldron-shaped, or bell-shaped as well.

Since the mortar and pestle were commonly used in apothecaries for crushing herbs and materials used in medicinal remedies, they are an icon of healing. Mortars and pestles are made of stone, marble, granite, or soapstone. In addition to crushing herbs, the mortar and pestle can be used to crush small crystal flakes, incense, minerals, shells, or resins. As you use the mortar and pestle for crushing herbs or other items, concentrate on what you plan to use the items for when putting them to use in Magickal applications; doing so allows you to add the additional energies of your intentions into the ingredients you are crushing.

A mortar and pestle, like the chalice, is symbolic of the Great Rite or the union of the God and Goddess; the mortar symbolizes the womb of the Goddess, and the pestle is a phallic symbol representing the God. Lore in Russia tells of Baba Yaga the Crone flying through the air in a mortar and pestle; these tools are symbolic of healing and this connects the crone image of the feminine with the healing arts.

Making it Magickal

Cleanse, bless, consecrate, and charge the mortar and pestle before using them. If you have a wooden mortar and pestle, you can paint or carve symbols on the exterior of the item. You can also purchase a set with Magickal symbols already on the item.

Care, Maintenance, and Cautions

Make sure that you clean the mortar and pestle thoroughly after each use. Typically, lukewarm water and a mild dish detergent are ideal cleaning agents for your mortar and pestle. Do not overzealously crush or pound materials in the mortar with the pestle. When not in use, make sure they are stored in a safe place; if positioned on an elevated area, make sure the mortar and pestle are not at risk of being nudged from the surface where they are stored.

For the Crafty Witch

If you do not have a mortar and pestle, and you need to crush herbs, you can put the herbs in a thick plastic bag and crush them with a rolling pin. You can also use a food processor to grind up leaves or roots. If you have a metal ladle, you can use the backside of the ladle to crush down herbs as well. If you are looking to crush up small crystals, you can wrap them in a cloth and gently strike the cloth with a hammer to reduce the crystals into a powdery substance.

Poppets

Description, Uses, and Symbolism

The term *poppet* is derived from the Old English word *popet* meaning "doll"; the term is also derived from the Latin *pupa*, meaning "chrysalis."[16] The connection of the word *poppet* with *pupa* may connote the chrysalis-like or shell-like nature of a poppet before it is Magickally transformed into the effigy of an individual. A poppet is a doll for the purpose of representing a specific individual or the effigy of a person.[17] Poppets are made from a variety of materials including paper, branches, clay, wax, wood, cloth, and carved roots. When an action is performed on a poppet, the action is also performed on an individual via the act of transference through sympathetic Magick. While many associate the use of poppets with Voodoo practices, their use is an ancient practice in a variety of cultures around the world.

Making it Magickal

You should name the doll after the individual you are working the healing Magick for and you should visualize the purpose as you make the poppet. As you visualize the purpose, you can capture the "essence" of the individual in your mind and direct that essence into the doll as you establish the psychic energies of the working at hand. Saying the person's name aloud is also helpful; a person's name conjures up the essence of the individual. You can use something personal belonging to the individual to add to the poppet you create, like a piece of hair trimming, a ribbon that belongs to them, or a photo of the individual. After you create the poppet, bless and consecrate the doll. You can then work healing Magick with the doll serving as the representation of the individual you want to heal.

Care, Maintenance, and Cautions

When making a poppet of cloth, make sure you do not cut yourself when cutting the fabric, and be careful as you stitch it together. Keep in mind that a poppet is a Magickal replica, so whatever happens to the doll can happen to the person it represents. Therefore, you must keep the poppet in a safe place at all times.

For the Crafty Witch

When you make a poppet, you can add herbs and crystals, aligned with your intentions, while filling it. For example, if you create a poppet for the purposes of promoting sobriety for someone battling an addiction, you can sew a small amethyst inside the doll, since the stone offers energies that help when one is attempting to heal addictions. You can also create clothing for the doll out of old clothing that belongs to the person the doll is supposed to represent, or you can create the doll out of fabric with colors that are chosen specifically for their energy vibrations.

Libation Vessel

Description, Uses, and Symbolism

A libation vessel is a container used for pouring liquid in order to pay reverence to the Divine by offering a libation. Like placing objects in an offering bowl, when liquid is poured into a libation vessel, the essence of the liquid is offered up to the Divine as of way of expressing gratitude. The Ancient Egyptians used libation vessels or buckets as is indicated by some archeological findings from the Pre-dynastic period; the buckets or vessels were used for making offerings of wines, oils, and spices and the offerings were made to deities or given as gifts to the recently deceased.[18] In Ancient Greece, an object called a *phiale* was used for the purposes of libation; the vessel was made of metal and had a bowl shape with a shallow cavity inside.[19] The Ancient Grecians also used *rhytons* or drinking horns for the purposes of liquid libation.[20] The *phiale* is more like the modern offering bowl today, while the *rhyton* is more like the modern libation vessel. A libation vessel typically has an area where liquid can be poured into the vessel and a hole in the bottom of the container so that the liquid can be easily poured into the earth or into the mouth of those that are partaking of libation.

Making it Magickal

No matter what vessel you choose for a libation vessel, cleanse, bless, consecrate, and charge it.

Care, Maintenance, and Cautions

After each libation, wash the vessel, periodically cleanse, and consecrate it. When placing the vessel outdoors, consider the fact that sweet liquids can draw ants and other critters to the area: this is why keeping the vessel clean is important, but you should regularly clean up the area where you pour your libations as well.

For the Crafty Witch

You can use something as simple as a terra cotta pot to make a libation vessel for outdoors. The pot already has a drainage hole where the libation liquid can escape and enter into the earth. You should paint the interior of the pot with a couple of coats of glaze; this will keep the porous pot from becoming stained while simultaneously making it easier to clean.

Potion Bottles

Description, Uses, and Symbolism

The term potion is rooted in the Latin *potare* meaning "to drink" and *potabilis,* meaning drinkable; it is also loosely rooted to the Latin *potio* meaning "poisonous drink."[21] A potion is a liquid that one consumes orally in order to derive the Magickal or healing benefits from the concoction. Potion bottles are needed if you plan to make any potions out of herbs. Colored bottles are sometimes required in order to maintain the potency of the potion you create. Amber and cobalt blue bottles help to keep a potion protected from being exposed to light that may diminish the potency of the potion in question. Clear bottles are only appropriate for use with potions that will not be affected by exposure to light.

Making it Magickal

Once you have chosen your potion bottles, cleanse, bless, consecrate and charge them; this is particularly true if you use antique bottles or if you buy bottles from the store. Remove any existing or residual energies from the bottles before using them.

Care, Maintenance, and Cautions

If you like, you can also use antique bottles for storing your potions; just remember that any embellishments you make to an antique may diminish the antique's value. Also, remember that you will need bottles with stoppers or caps so you can keep your potions from evaporating or spilling. Make sure that if you reuse any potion bottles you own that you clean them thoroughly, especially if you use them for different potions. When making potions, always research ingredients to ensure their safety for ingestion or use.

For the Crafty Witch

You can buy decorated potion bottles or get plain bottles and decorate them. You can also make your own potions. If you enjoy making potions, you can add your favorite recipes to your *grimoire* or create a separate book that is solely dedicated to all of your favorite concoctions.

Protection Pots

Description, Uses, and Symbolism

A protection pot is a vessel or container that stores items that you charge with the task of protection. This tool is very versatile, allowing you to use any kind of bowl, pot, or container, and to charge whatever items you like to serve for the purposes of protection. Gather rocks from outdoors, clean them, and charge each one individually to create the protection pot. You can also use things like acorns, seashells, glass stones, or large beads. The protection pot is akin to a witch's bottle, only you do not hide the protection pot, and you do not have to bury it. In fact, you can place it anywhere in the home to derive its protective properties, but it is best if it is placed on a porch or nearby the entryway of your home.

Making it Magickal

Decorate the vessel or pot that you choose, thereby adding your own essence to the vessel. Cleanse, bless, consecrate, and charge the pot with protective energies. You will also want to cleanse, bless, and consecrate the stones you put in the vessel before you charge them for the purposes of protection.

Care, Maintenance, and Cautions

If you place the protection pot near your front door, make sure you put it in an area where it will not be knocked over. In addition, if you decide to add herbs to the pot, make sure that the pot is not in a place where it can be easily reached by your animals or children; many herbs are poisonous. In addition, the stones inside the pot can present a choking hazard for small children.

For the Crafty Witch

If you do not want to take the time to make a protection pot, you can charge other objects for the purposes of home protection. If you have a favorite statue, chimes, stones, plants, or other objects you enjoy, you can charge them for protection and position them near doorways in the home as well. You will need a glass, ceramic, clay, or metal container. Any size container will do as long as the container is made from natural materials from the earth and that it is not made from plastic or other synthetic materials.

Protection Pot Spell

You will need a pile of stones gathered from outdoors or small glass stones as the object you will charge for the purposes of protection. After you decorate the pot or vessel to your preference, take each stone that will be placed in the pot one by one. Place the stone in your receptive hand and cover it with your projective hand while you say the following:

> I charge stone on this day,
> Keep me safe both night and day.

As an alternative, you can say the following words:

> With these spoken words of power,
> These stones protect me every hour.

Place the charged stone in the container and repeat the process with every stone until the pot is full. Position your pot by the front door or in another area where you want to instill protective energies. You can renew this spell to recharge the stones for protection once every six months or annually if you desire.

Sigils

Description, Uses, and Symbolism

The term *sigil* comes from the Latin word *sigillum* meaning "signature or seal."[22] A sigil is a symbol, icon, or emblem created with a specific purpose, usually for protection. Sigils are simple or intricate designs used for a specific purpose. Sigils are like compact signs or symbols containing layers of meaning that are further empowered by your will and intent as you create them. Some sigils are the symbol of a specific entity or deity. You would use sigils to call upon the deity, entity, or specific energies. Other sigils can be used for protection when you carry them with you. Some sigils can be buried at the four corners of one's property for protection purposes. Renaissance grimoires are inundated with an array of different sigils, all with different meanings and purposes.

Making it Magickal

Many sigils are ancient designs; they can be made on parchment, paper, or engraved in an object. Whatever symbols you use or sigils you create make sure you consecrate, bless, and charge them before use.

Care, Maintenance, and Cautions

When you make sigils, make sure you thoroughly understand the symbols you are using and what they mean. Likewise, if you copy sigils from another source, again it is imperative that you understand what the sigil is used for and the image's meaning. Otherwise, you can end up with an outcome that you might not have anticipated. In addition, be fully aware of your inner intentions, both conscious and subconscious, before you begin working with sigils for any reason.

For the Crafty Witch

When making sigils, use parchment if you desire. If you want to empower the sigils with your energies to an even greater degree, you can even make your own paper. You can also use colored inks to make sigils to lend the color's vibrational energies to the working at hand. When drawing sigils, consider using calligraphy pen and inks as well; it takes a greater deal of concentration to use a calligraphy pen and ink, and the additional concentration will further empower the sigils you are creating.

Statues

Description, Uses, and Symbolism

The term *statue* comes from the Latin word *statua* meaning "standing image" and the word *status* meaning "to stare, position, or standing."[23] Many pagans use statues of different animal totems and deities; the statues serve as the effigy or image of whatever the statue represents. There are hundreds of statues that you can buy, and the price of a statue varies depending upon the size, complexity, and the materials used in the creation of the statues you choose.

Making it Magickal

Cleanse, bless, and consecrate the statue. You can also give small gifts to the Divine by embellishing the statue of your choice with crystals, small jewels, or additional ornamentations. Put your statue in a place of honor, like your altar room or on your altar.

Care, Maintenance, and Cautions

Many statues are made of a poly resin material, which easily cracks and breaks if you accidentally bump the item into other objects or if it falls. You should put the statue in a safe place where it will not be nudged off the edge of a shelf or table.

For the Crafty Witch

If you are into sculpture or you like working with clay, make your own statues or replicas of your patron deities. If you do not have the funds to invest in statues, you can get posters or pictures of your patron deities as well. If you like to draw, create depictions of the deities that appeal to you. Some statues are plain, so if you desire, you can paint them or embellish them with your choice of décor as well.

Witch's Jar or Bottle

Description, Uses, and Symbolism

According to some superstitions, a witch's jar or witch's bottle was at one time used for retaliation against someone who was believed to have bewitched another, or for the purposes of warding off the workings of witchcraft.[24] Another superstition asserted that you could render a witch immobile if you added her urine to a bottle containing nails and pins and then set the bottle and its contents on fire.[25] Witch bottle lore may also be loosely related to the superstition that one could discover the identity of a witch by suspending a bottle in the home of a person who the witch allegedly bewitched; when the bewitched hung the bottle from the chimney in the home, the witch would appear and request its removal.[26] Today, a witch's jar or bottle is something else entirely, and it is much like a protection pot in that it is used for the purposes of protection. This type of bottle not only protects the maker of the bottle, but everything in the home or on the property; what's more, the bottle serves as a repellent for any kind of negative energies.

There are different kinds of witch's bottles; you can make one out of a long necked bottle or regular canning jar. As long as you can seal the jar, it is useful for making a witch's bottle. Ancient bottles were filled with pins, rusty or bent nails, razor blades, and sometimes urine, but modern day witch's bottles contain things like thread, herbs, shells, sea salt, wine, sand, fresh earth, consecrated salt water, stones, and crystals.

Making it Magickal

Cleanse, bless, consecrate, and charge the jar before you fill it with the materials you choose. You can give an extra seal to the jar by applying melted wax around the lid. Many practitioners assert that a witch's bottle needs to be buried once it is created; you can bury it in the woods a distance from your home, or you can bury it on your property. If you do not have a place to bury the jar, you can store it in your home, but you will want to hide it away in a place where it will not be easily seen.

Care, Maintenance, and Cautions

If you choose sharp objects to put in the jar, take considerable care as you place them inside the bottle so you do not cut yourself. Rusty objects are not recommended, but if you do decide to use them, make sure you are up to date on your Tetanus vaccination. Keep your bottle well hidden; if it is seen or tampered with, you will have to make another and discard the one you have already made.

For the Crafty Witch

To enhance the protective energies of the witch's bottle, use bottles made of colored glass; make sure that the bottle's color aligns with the Magick you are working. You can also paint the exterior of the bottle with symbols of protection. Instead of herbs, you have the alternative of adding essential oils too. To empower the bottle you make with your personal power, add a snippet of your own hair to whatever additional materials you include inside it.

More Essentials: Herbs, Stones, Oils, and Incense

Herbs

Many witches use herbs for cooking, spells and for the purposes of natural healing. There are many wonderful books you can use to find out more about herbs and their Magickal properties. What we offer you here is some of the basic considerations to keep in mind as you begin to think about using herbs for Magickal applications or for healing.

- First, even if you have one or two herbal references to use, make sure you do your homework when it comes time to learn about an herb's properties. Don't be in a rush to use an herb just because one or two books suggest that the herbs are good for dealing with a certain condition or malady; you may be missing out on vital information related to interactions and potential side effects.
- Do not mistake information in an herbal guide for medical advice. Further, if you have questions about an herb's properties, do not use it until you speak with another, more skilled practitioner or an herbal specialist.
- Follow the instructions for herbal use to the letter; do not assume that the more you use the greater the result will be; this is particularly true if you are planning to ingest the herbs you have chosen. Furthermore, if you plan to consume any herbs, whether it is a supplement, the raw herb, or a decoction, make sure you talk with your doctor first; the physician can alert you to any potential interactions you might face or any allergic reactions you should watch out for when using herbs.
- Some herbs are good for long-term use and others are not. Make sure you research how long it is safe to use an herb in addition to what dosage you should use.
- We do not recommend that pregnant women or nursing mothers use herbs at all. There is insufficient data as to whether or not herbal solutions are harmful to the fetus, and consumed herbs can sometimes pass from mother to child during the process of nursing. We recommend that until you are no longer nursing or pregnant that you forgo the use of herbs entirely, even if the herb is only a dietary supplement.
- Some herbs can cause light sensitivity in some people too; if you are photosensitive, you will need to check on the herbal solutions you make to ensure you do not have a negative reaction.
- Some herbal solutions can affect your blood, and therefore should not be used in conjunction with blood thinners. In addition, there are herbs that can augment the immune system; if you have an overactive immune system, refrain from using immune system triggering solutions. Meanwhile, there are herbs that can have a negative impact on your blood sugar levels; diabetics need to be very careful about the herbs that they consume.
- There are some herbs that have mind-altering effects; these herbs may or may not be acceptable natural treatments for people with a mental illness. Again, consulting a physician before herbal use is advised.

A Note on Harvesting and Collecting from Nature

When harvesting herbs for ritual or spell use, it is always important to consider the fragile condition of our Mother Earth and to heed the lesson of "fairly take and fairly give." More importantly, always be ready to do your part in preserving and promoting balance on the Earth. Whenever you are harvesting herbs, either out in nature or those you have grown on your own, it is never acceptable to take more than you need to use or than you plan to share with others. You should not acquire herbs or animal totems from endangered species. As you harvest herbs, make sure you thank the plant or tree for their gift to you, and use only what you will need. If it is at all possible, use what has fallen to the ground first before you harvest from the plant or tree as well. The needs of the Earth must always come before a desire to have the most potent spell or dream pillow. Likewise, using fur from an endangered animal to make a ritual tool does not make the tool any more powerful than it would be without the animal fur in question.

Stones

Stones and crystals are also vital tools for the modern-day witch; there are so many stones to choose from that describing the varieties is beyond the scope of this book. There are myriad guides on the healing and energetic properties of crystals that you can use in determining what stones you should use for specific purposes. You can sometimes find natural quartz or rose quartz in stones outdoors, and you can even tumble your own stones if you desire. You will also find plenty of selection in terms of stones to purchase in stone shops, in hobby shops, and online. Some stones are associated with specific months, cardinal directions, deities, planets, and Magickal purposes.

Whatever stones you choose, remember to cleanse, bless, consecrate, and charge them for your Magickal workings. When you want to clean a stone and make it look its best, you can run the stone under cold water and dry it. If you use a cleaning product, you will find that it diminishes the stone's natural shine. You can then charge them by exposing them to full moon energies for three days, followed by the act of physically charging them yourself. If small enough, you can also bury the stones in a bowl of sea salt for a few days. Allowing the stones to sit on your altar allows the stone to accumulate raised energies from ritual workings too.

Chapter 3
Meditation Tools

"Anytime we are fully present in the moment we are meditating."
—Joan Borysenko

Meditation Hints

Making meditation part of your daily practices is a must for every Witch. Meditation offers health benefits, helps to expand the mind, and improves psychic and/or intuitive abilities. Meditation readies the mind for the day-to-day decisions you will have to make, and allows you to become fully aware and present of the immediate moment. When you meditate regularly, you will achieve greater concentration and focus; this will lend to your ability to perform more powerful rituals and spells.

You have to meditate more than a few times to gain any advantages from the practice. Dedicate yourself to the practice daily. If possible, commit to meditating at a specific time each day. Even if you have a very busy schedule, you can still practice meditation for five or ten minutes in the morning before you begin your day. Look at meditation as, not a temporary technique for achieving a goal, but a practice that you will make part of your life for the rest of your life. Even if you are not feeling well, you will find that the act of meditating can help you in healing.

Before you settle down to meditate, you can benefit from doing a couple of body stretches. As you stretch your muscles, you can immediately alleviate tension, making it easier for you to relax. Once you are fully relaxed, you can sit in a comfortable position. Do not worry so much about the proper position to sit in, but do concern yourself with having good posture and keeping your spinal column aligned.

Choose your favorite incense and light it for your meditation sessions. Scents help in altering your state of consciousness, your mood, and make it easier to relax. The scent of incense as it burns allows you to begin focusing on the breath since sweet smelling incense makes it even more pleasurable to draw in each breath. When you meditate, you want your heart rate and breathing to slow down. You need to focus on drawing in positive energies when you inhale, and expelling negative every time you exhale.

For your first few meditations, your goal will be to quiet your thoughts, a process far more complex than you might imagine. Many people meditating for the first time have difficulty preventing intrusive thoughts from invading their mind. The act of clearing the mind becomes even more difficult if you are already being distracted by pressure driven thoughts related to daily obligations or emotional upsets. As you meditate, every time an invasive thought comes along, simply ignore the thought and re-center your focus. You can refocus on breathing when an intrusive thought arises and each time another thought intrudes on your meditation, return your thoughts to the breathing process. Eventually, calming the mind will become more natural to you.

Meditation: What to Avoid

If you are new to meditation, avoid trying to force your focus; at first, you will find it difficult to keep your mind free from distractions. Forcing the issue will only result in frustration. Keep your meditation sessions brief, at least at the beginning, until you become accustomed to meditating. Do not be in a rush to achieve the ideal meditative state; through repetition, you will eventually master the art.

Do not become overly relaxed when you meditate. If you are lying down or reclining, you are more likely to doze off instead of alter your state of awareness the way you desire. In fact, if you are exhausted, do not meditate at all; you are far more likely to drift off to sleep. When you are new to meditation, it is best to perform the practice while you are sitting up: This will reduce the likelihood of becoming too relaxed, but it will allow you to relax enough so that you can fully engross yourself in the practice.

When meditating, make sure you wear non-restrictive attire. You do not want to be physically uncomfortable during your session. This does not mean you have to have fancy clothing to meditate; if you are comfortable in sweat pants and a sweat shirt then, by all means, wear them during your practice.

One of the biggest downfalls you will face when you try to meditate is unnecessary distractions. Find a quite space where you can meditate: Your sacred space where your altar is established is a good place for meditating, or you might even want to set up a miniature meditation altar. If you live with other people, make sure to let them know what you are doing and that you do not want to be disturbed. You should also turn off any electronics, and make the room as quiet as possible. If necessary, turn down the volume on your answering machine or take the phone off the hook. Turn off your cell phone, and do not feel guilty about taking a few minutes just for you. If you are new to meditation, begin with silent meditations before moving onto guided meditations or meditating with music. Surprisingly, as much as it is craved throughout a chaotic day, one of the hardest things to do is to grow accustomed to silence.

Meditative Tools

While it is true that you need nothing more than a quiet area and the willingness to meditate, you might benefit from using some of the meditation tools that are available. Many tools make it easier to concentrate, and work toward helping you enter into an altered state of awareness. Other tools enhance meditative techniques.

BackJacks

Description, Uses, and Symbolism

Backjacks are special chairs that you can use during your meditation session. The seats have steel frames covered with cushioning made out of soft, durable materials. Backjacks, after assembly, are positioned on the floor and used to support the back while sitting or reclining. The chair has an upside down "T" shape when it is in the seated position; the bottom portion of the seat has extra padding to make sitting in the chair comfortable, and the back of the chair is high so that it supports the entire back up to the shoulders. The chair is portable; it can be used indoors or out.

Backjacks are outstanding tools for ensuring proper posture when you are meditating. Since the chairs help keep your posture straight, they can be used to ensure that you practice your breathing techniques correctly; you will be able to breathe more deeply when your spine is straight and your diaphragm is not being compressed due to an overly relaxed posture. If you are just starting out with meditation, you should use the backjack in the upright position: this will ensure that you do not become too relaxed or that you fall asleep during the meditation. As you become more skilled with your practice, you can use the backjack to support your back as you recline.

If you are not used to keeping your posture straight, you may experience back strain or achiness as you meditate. The backjack is a tool that can be used to alleviate the strain, since it lends your back additional support; you can use the backjack to help straighten your spine until your back muscles are strong enough to maintain the correct meditation posture for longer periods.

Making it Magickal

If you want to make the seat look more witchy, you can use fabric paints to add designs to the seat; you can add symbols like spirals, triple moons, triquetras, pentacles, and yin-yangs. Unless the seat has been exposed to negative energies, there is no need to consecrate or bless the tool, but you can occasionally smudge the seat to ensure it maintains the appropriate energies.

Care, Maintenance, and Cautions

You might want to invest in replacement covers to help keep the original fabric of the backjack clean. You will need to wipe down the steel-tube frame of the chair occasionally: You do not need special metal cleaners to so. Washing the seating is not recommended: This can cause the seating to lose some of its rigidity and shape, thereby ruining the chair.

If you consider buying a backjack, find out if the backjack is a stackable chair or a folding unit; not all backjacks can be folded up and stored away. If you are considering a chair for meditation sessions while you travel, you will benefit from getting a foldable version. If you do take them along with you on vacation, or if you choose to meditate near a lake, river, or beach, you should not use the chair while wearing damp clothing; doing so can cause the chair to mildew.

For the Crafty Witch

If you have a gaming chair, it can serve as a backjack. You can also use a beanbag to relax in as you meditate, instead of a backjack; however, you will not get as much support for your posture. The chairs are offered in a range of sizes; for adults, the best option is the extra large backjacks. The chairs are actually comprised of pieces of steel that are connected; a cover is then slid over the top of the connected steel pieces to make the chair. You also have the option of using meditation mats, benches, or you can choose a comfortable chair or couch. Alternatively, some people prefer to use zafus (small round pillows) and zafutons (rectangular soft pads) for seating purposes during meditation.

If you are skilled at sewing, you can make your own backjack chair covers to place over the original padded cover out of whatever material you desire. While comfort will be of foremost concern, you can still choose a pattern, design, or print of your preference. You might want to choose fabric colors that match the décor of the area where you meditate, or you can match the fabric to colors that make you think of peace and tranquility. Alternatively, you can drape decorative scarves over the chair with colors that lend calming energies to meditation practices.

Chimes

Description, Uses, and Symbolism

The etymology of the term *chime* is unclear; it is possible the word was at one time *chymbe* or *chimb*, both of which are a distortion of *cymbale*, derived from the Latin *cymbalum* for cymbal.[1] Wind chimes or wind-bells, are made of suspended objects, aluminum tubing, bamboo, brass, ceramic, copper, glass, pewter, stained glass, wood, metal, or other materials. When the wind blows through the suspended chimes, the objects clank together and offer up a harmonious, musical sound. The type of material used to create wind chimes has a direct effect on the sound produced.

The sound generated from wind chimes can vary: you can get soprano, mezzo-soprano, bass, alto, and tenor chimes. Wind chimes are much like bells in that they help alleviate negative or stagnant energies. Alternatively, automatic meditation timers offer an extended period of silence, interrupted by the sound of a chime, bell, gong, or a singing bowl to signal the completion of your meditation. An automatic chime meditation timer is a special device that can be set to chime at a specified time automatically. The hand-held chime is a device that can be placed in the hands or on the table: it comes with a mallet for striking the device when desired.

Making it Magickal

Suspend your chimes in and around your sacred space. If you charge them for protection, they can serve the dual purpose of protecting your sacred space and offering up melodic sounds during ritual workings. You can do the same with your outdoor chimes; charge them to protect the exterior of your home.

Care, Maintenance, and Cautions

If you invest in an automatic timer, follow the care instructions provided with the device, and change the battery occasionally to prevent the device from freezing or malfunctioning. No matter what kind of chimes you invest in, use the appropriate cleaning materials to keep the chimes in good condition. Use a wood polish to clean bamboo or chimes made of wood, and gun oil is excellent for giving bronze, copper, pewter, stainless steel, and aluminum a high shine. Clean stained glass and ceramic chimes with regular glass cleaner or white vinegar diluted in water. Do not use abrasive scrubbers on wind chimes; make sure you use a soft cloth to prevent scratching the surface of the chime parts. Finally, if you choose to display/use your wind chimes outdoors, take them down when you anticipate severe weather.

If you use an automatic meditation timer, put it in a safe place, on a solid, level surface, to avoid accidentally damaging the device. Use the same care with your hand chime. Alternatively, outdoor chimes sometimes require periodic untangling to the exposure to rough winds; be gentle as you untangle them so they do not break. Indoor chimes do not usually have the same problem, but they can prove problematic if you suspend them low in a high traffic area of the home. When suspending your chimes outside, make sure that there is enough room for the chimes to move freely when they are affected by the winds; they should not collide with the exterior of your home or into other objects nearby.

For the Crafty Witch

There are online meditation timers you can use if you do not want to invest in a chime timer; some allow you to choose the sound that plays, and the frequency of the chime. You can also download free or fee-based chimes sound tracks to an mp3 player. You can get a chime meditation phone app for your mobile phone.

You can make wind chimes out of copper tubing, aluminum tubing, shells, or terra-cotta pots. You can create a wind chime header out of a piece of wood. If you use clay pots, get several small pots of varying sizes. Design the pots any way you desire: Consider adding pentacles, suns, moons, stars, a witch's conical hat, or other witchy designs to the exterior of each pot with acrylic paints. Mix and match your designs to your preference. Make sure you use a gloss coat to keep the paint from chipping. If you use shells, you can alternate the shells with beads to create interesting designs. Suspend the objects you choose from fishing line or heavy twine at varying lengths, ensuring that the objects can gently strike one another when the wind blows.

Indoor / Outdoor Fountains

Description, Uses, and Symbolism

A water fountain can have a simple or ornate design; fountains are closed systems consisting of one or more basins and pumps that generate and recycle water in order to produce a continuous stream. A fountain varies in terms of size and materials used to create the fountain. Fountains are made of copper, cast stone, slate, marble, granite, glass, or stainless steel, among other materials. You can choose from tabletop, wall, floor, or outdoor variants. Fountains may also have special features like chimes, bells, gongs, lighting, or one or more places to position tea light candles.

Fountains symbolize the source of life. The waters represent the streaming nature of consciousness and the depth of the subconscious. The sound of flowing water signals thoughts of peace, calming, tranquility, abundance, fertility, and prosperity. Fountains also symbolize the bubbling, endless well of creativity and inspiration. Since water can come from deep within the earth, flowing water represents the flow of human emotions, deep, hidden mysteries, and the Divine Feminine. The use of fountains during meditation allows for you to alter your state of consciousness, to connect to the feminine aspect of the divine, and to master important spiritual lessons like how to move, act, and react like flowing water in everyday situations.

Making it Magickal

You can use consecrated water to make the fountain a Magickal tool; however, do not use consecrated salt water since the salt will clog the fountain's pump. You can Magickally charge the fountain so that as the water flows in the fountain, it can keep positive energies flowing in your home and sacred space.

Care, Maintenance, and Cautions

Whether you have an indoor or outdoor fountain, you will find it is subject to the accumulation of minerals, this will appear as a white residue on the fountain's components: The residue can be removed with a lime remover. The fountain pump has to be cleaned once a month: this can be accomplished by soaking the pump in several cups of white vinegar diluted in a gallon of fresh water. You can soak the pump for fifteen or twenty minutes to ensure it is free from algae or mineral build up. If you are using a small indoor fountain, add about a tablespoon of bleach to the water to keep it odor free or from stagnating too quickly. Some outdoor fountains require the application of paint and a sealer every few years.

Failure to maintain adequate water levels in your fountain will result in pump failure. The pump always has to be fully submersed in water. Resist the urge to add decorative components to the water in a fountain: adding things like glitter and small beads makes the water look nice, but it can damage the pump. If you have a water fountain outdoors, it has to be drained during the winter; if the water is allowed to freeze, it could crack the fountain. Indoor fountains should be kept in an area where pets cannot access them.

For the Crafty Witch

If you love the sound of running water, but you don't want to deal with maintaining a fountain, you can invest in a sound maker capable of generating the sound of rainwater, storms, streams, rivers, and fountains. You can also go to a nearby lake, river, or beach and record the natural sounds of the water to play back during your meditations.

You can make an indoor fountain out of vases, urns, bamboo, and terra-cotta bowls or pots; if you choose pots, make sure they are absent of a drainage hole. You will have to invest in a pump, and hoses. You will also require rocks, glass stones or other ornamentations to fill the fountain with when you have completed its construction. Alternatively, you can create your own outdoor fountain in your backyard: Once completed, the area can serve as an ideal place for meditation sessions. If you already have a pond in your yard, it is a great place to establish a natural outdoor waterfall.

Gongs and Singing Bowls

Description, Uses, and Symbolism

The gong is a discoid-shaped percussion instrument named after the resonant sound it produces. A gong is commonly suspended from an open framed gong stand and is a metal instrument often made of tin, brass, or a copper alloy.[2] The instrument is struck by a hammer or mallet in order to generate sound. Singing bowls are crafted of metal and can be struck on the side of the bowl with the head or the end of the gong hammer to produce a gong-like sound. You can strike a gong at the beginning of your meditation, several times during your meditation, or to signal your mind that you are finished with a meditation. Gongs can also be used to announce the beginning or the ending of Magickal rites, and sometimes they are placed at the entrance of outdoor labyrinths, so that they can be used to invoke a higher state of awareness.

Making it Magickal

If you have a small tabletop gong and enough room on the altar, you can leave the gong on the altar all the time: this will allow the tool to be charged with ritual energies. Larger gongs can be kept in your sanctuary to achieve the same outcome. You can use incense to bless the gong; since a gong is an air tool, using incense like Nag Champa, Myrrh, Sage, Frankincense, Dragon's Blood, Lavender, Night Bloom, or Jasmine to bless it is ideal. You can dedicate the tool to a specific deity like Kwan Yin as well.

Care, Maintenance, and Cautions

It does not take much to produce sound from a gong; therefore, there is no reason to strike the gong with excessive force to generate a sound. If you strike the gong too hard, you run the risk of producing a very loud sound. The larger the gong is in terms of size, the louder and more unsettling the sound can be. You also run the risk of knocking the gong off balance and potentially breaking it if it falls from an elevated place, like a stand or table.

For the Crafty Witch

Instead of a gong, you can use a bell or a set of chimes in order to produce a sound. You can also get a CD with gong or singing bowl sounds.

You can use a single piece cake/pie tin to make a homemade gong. If the cake/pie tin does not have a hole in it, you can drill one or two in the handle. You can use a piece of twine to slip through the drilled holes in order hang the gong from a hook: either one you attach to a surface like a wall or one you insert in the ground. You can paint the gong with acrylics, provided you also finish it off with a coat of polyurethane. You can purchase a small rubber mallet, or you can make one out of a wooden dowel. Alternatively, an investment in a small, wooden, kitchen mallet can give you a tool that can also be used as a gong hammer.

Guided Meditations

Description, Uses, and Symbolism

Guided meditations are narrated scripts that prompt the meditative process in a systematic manner. You can have another person guide you through a meditation or you can use a recorded meditation. Some guided meditations have music in the background and/or subliminal messages as well.

Making it Magickal

If you create meditations, you can write meditations that allow you to focus on animal totems, Tarot images, candles, Magickal objects, symbols, colors, spiritual questions, or personal concerns. You can also write lengthy meditations related to meeting your spirit guides, releasing negative emotions, overcoming obstacles impeding your spiritual growth, past life regression, or astral travel. Use your favorite incense or use scents conducive to meditation like Amber, Bergamot, Cypress, Cedar, Frankincense, Jasmine, Juniper Berry, Lavender, Lily, Lotus, Patchouli, Rose, Rosemary, Rosewood, Sage, Sweetgrass, Vanilla, Ylang Ylang, or Opium.

Care, Maintenance, and Cautions

If you have guided meditations stored on CDs or audio tapes, keep them in cases to ensure their longevity. Make sure you fully understand the subliminal messages in a guided meditation before you use it. If you buy a CD with guided meditations, make sure you like the music and the vocalizations. You will have a hard time meditating if you find the music or the voice that is guiding you irritating.

For the Crafty Witch

If you find meditations that you like in books, you can record them to a digital recorder and create your own CD of guided meditations. You can use a tape recorder and an audio cassette to make your own guided meditation tapes.

You can also experiment with playing different background music or sounds as your record your favorite meditations. You can write your own meditations from scratch and record them for later use.

Labyrinth

Description, Uses, and Symbolism

A labyrinth is a structure consisting of a complex passage; the Egyptians created these structures and they are mentioned in Greek myth. The labyrinth is most often associated with the Greek Minotaur, particularly the labyrinth near Cnossus in Crete that, according to myth, was created for King Minos by Dadelalus upon the king's orders to create a structure to confine the Minotaur. [3] The association of the term "labyrinth" with the housing of the Minotaur is rather odd considering that a labyrinth is a path consisting of a single, clear path in and out of the structure. The "labyrinth" serving as the home of the Minotaur was a maze, not a labyrinth, consisting of many paths; the structure was purposely designed to confuse and trap the Minotaur inside it. The distinction between the labyrinth and a maze is incredibly important; a maze confuses the individual that walks it, while a single-pathed labyrinth, with only one way in and one way out, is a journey of enlightenment.

The labyrinth is another exceptional meditation tool. You can either walk the labyrinth outdoors or use a smaller version printed on a floor mat so you can perform the journey indoors. The labyrinth symbolizes the depth of the human mind as well as a journey into your subconscious. The image of the labyrinth from above looks somewhat similar to the drawing of the brain. The path represents the journey inward to reconnect with the Divine and the self. It can also symbolize the journey you make through life from youth to eldership. The labyrinth symbolizes transformation; upon entering, walking, and exiting the labyrinth, you are spiritually transformed. The labyrinth even symbolizes birth and rebirth, as some consider the labyrinth a symbolic representation of the Goddess's womb. Those who walk the labyrinth can do so while seeking inner guidance, insight, inspiration, epiphanies, or to trigger creativity.

Making it Magickal

The act of creating a labyrinth is a Magickal act. If you have an outdoor labyrinth, allowing more people to walk the path makes the sacred site more powerful. In an outdoor setting, add candles, statues, and decorative items that represent the four elements. In the center of the labyrinth, you have the option of adding a small altar where you can make offerings to the Divine or where you can keep an eternal flame lit.

Care, Maintenance, and Cautions

If you have an outdoor labyrinth maintain the area by keeping the labyrinth's path free from weeds and obstacles. If you have constructed the labyrinth out of stones, occasionally re-position the stones so that the path of the labyrinth remains clear. When establishing an altar in the center, make sure you clean it on a regular basis.

With outdoor labyrinths, make sure the path is wide enough so that you prevent potential falls or injuries as you walk the path. If you set up candles around the labyrinth, indoors or out, make sure you snuff them out before you leave the area. Do not allow anyone with negative energies to walk your labyrinth; this can taint the energies of the area and lower the vibration.

For the Crafty Witch

You can print out a labyrinth from an online drawing and trace the path with a pencil or your finger. Alternatively, for labyrinths established outdoors, you have the option of planting floral arrangements outside the outer ring of the labyrinth. You can also create a labyrinth out of hedges; bear in mind, however, that the hedges will require regular pruning. If you opt for hedges, you can add white or colored outdoor lights to the hedges to give them an additional, Magickal effect.

Mala Beads

Description, Uses, and Symbolism

Mala beads are strings of rosary beads, sometimes identified as a *japa-māla,* meaning "prayer necklace."[4] In Burmese Buddhism, the rosary is referred to as *Tsi-puthi,* meaning "mind garland."[5] Most mala beads consist of 108 beads. Smaller quarter mala beads have 27 beads. The beads are used for meditating, chanting, or while reciting mantras or divine names.[6] While these beads are used in Hindu and Buddhist practices, they can be used by anyone during meditation to improve concentration skills and to unify body and mind. The beads allow you to recite a specific number of chants or words without actually having to concentrate on counting: this allows your concentration to remain on the actual focus of the meditation.

Mala beads are made out of different materials including turquoise, agate, bone, amber, carnelian, amethyst, crystals, black onyx, tourmaline, jade, citrine, garnet, green fluorite, opals, clear and smoky quartz, pink lepidolite, purple fluorite, rose quartz, rosewood, sandalwood, olivewood, tiger eye, or mother of pearl. With regular use, mala beads can become a trigger for altering your state of awareness so that you are instantly ready for meditation. Rosary beads have different meanings depending upon the culture. In numerology, the sum of all of the digits in the number 108 also equals 9 (1 + 0 + 8 = 9); the Buddhists use the 108 beads to represent "the attributes of Buddha;" the beads have a numerological significance since 108 is a multiple of 9.[7] The beads also represent the 108 symbols on the footprints or soles of Buddha.[8] If you have a number that is particularly significant to you or that corresponds with Magickal workings, you can apply your own symbolic meaning to the beads you use.

Making it Magickal

You can also use mala beads for reciting daily affirmations. For example, when repeating an affirmation, you can move your thumb around the bead in a deosil direction for each affirmation you repeat. To meditate on a specific word or idea, you can come up with a short chant and use the mala beads to improve your concentration. You can wear the beads on your wrist or around your neck during ritual; this will instill ritual energies into the beads.

Care, Maintenance, and Cautions

If you choose to wear your mala beads on your neck or wrist, take care not to snag them on anything so you can keep the beads intact. Keep them free of negative energy; do not allow anyone with negative energies to handle them. If the beads are influenced by negative energies, run them under cold water to free them from the negative, then re-bless and re-consecrate them.

For the Crafty Witch

If you have a beaded necklace at home, you can use it as a set of mala beads. If you have a set of Mardi Gras beads, you can use those as well. Be aware that if you use a necklace or string of beads not originally intended for use as mala beads, the count of the beads may or may not be equal to a number divisible by nine.

As an alternative, try making your own mala beads by stringing beads of your choice together. You might like making several different sets for use during different meditations, too. Put beads on fishing line, hemp, or twine and make it to the length you desire. Add a single large bead, one bigger than all the rest of the beads you choose: this bead is the first to be strung onto your twine, string, or hemp. You can then put all of your smaller beads on the string; when you are finished, you can tie the twine or string together at the ends to form a loop or slip the end through the starter large bead and tie the beads off. You can also add a small tassel to the end of the loop if you desire.

Mandalas

Description, Uses, and Symbolism

The term *mandala* (pronounced *mun-du-la*) is Sanskrit meaning *totality* or *circle*. Mandalas are drawings consisting of a circle with interior geometrical designs. A mandala can represents sacred space, the Earth, the Moon, the Sun, the entire universe, and it is a symbol of completeness. The term *mandala* also describes a Magick circle.[9] You can create a mandala on any surface; the instant you do, you have established sacred space. Mandalas serve as a visual stimulus during meditation practices; you can look at and contemplate the intricate designs, colors, and structure of a mandala already completed or design your own. As you focus on the completed mandala your thoughts are focused on its design, and all other thoughts or distractions subside: As you create a mandala for yourself, your mind is focused on the visual experience, and the act of creation. Thus, the use of mandalas proves an ideal tool for those just starting out with meditative practices, and they are ideal for individuals adept in meditation since the use/creation of mandalas leads to a calmed and tranquil state.

Mandalas can serve as a creative method for finding the solution to a problem or it can also be used in healing practices. During the creation or coloring process, you can concentrate on a question or concern. It is helpful to have a notepad or a digital tape recorder nearby so that you can note any inspirational ideas, potential solutions, or epiphanies you come up with too.

Making it Magickal

Like the labyrinth, a mandala is sacred space the minute it is created. If you frame the mandala, you can hang it up to remind you of your spiritual journey, your spiritual goals, and your important role as a small part of the tapestry of creation.

Care, Maintenance, and Cautions

When you finish your mandalas, you might want to consider framing them to keep them protected. You can also put them into a scrapbook or photo album for safekeeping. You can use them again in the future for contemplation. However, in some traditions, the mandala is often disposed of once it has been finished; this is particularly true of sand mandalas. Once made, the sand mandala is destroyed as a representation of the evanescent, ephemeral, and transient nature of all things.

When designing Mandalas you will find that the designs are very intricate and completing the mandala can take several sessions. If you have a repetitive motion injury, especially one that affects the hands, wrists, arms, shoulders, or neck, you should not push yourself to finish a complex mandala in one session. Work only as long as you are comfortable, and complete the mandala over several sessions to avoid aggravating your condition or inducing further injury. You can also work with smaller mandalas that might not take as long to complete.

For the Crafty Witch

If you have access to the Internet, you can obtain thousands of different mandalas. If you are good at drawing, make your own mandalas and color them. If you do not have a penchant for sketch work, then there are books that offer templates that you can color. You can use any medium you desire to stylize your mandalas, including crayons, pencils, poster board paint, acrylics, pastels, oils, or you can use things you have collected from nature, like small flat stones, acorn tops, colorful leaves, flower petals, and pine needles. There are even software programs you can invest in if you are interested in graphically designing mandalas.

Sand Gardens / Zen Gardens

Description, Uses, and Symbolism

A sand garden is a form of *kare-sansui;* a garden consisting of fine sand, rocks, and decorative elements.[10] The sand in the garden symbolizes water, and the stones symbolize mountains. Zen Gardens or Sand Gardens are a beautiful way to calm the mind. The tabletop versions consist of a rectangular wooden basin, often made of rosewood. The interior of the box contains polished rocks and white sand. Sometimes other ornamentations are added, like ceramic cranes or swans, mini stone bridges, colorful pieces of cement, polished stones, or other decorative pieces. When purchased, these basins come with a small broom, a bamboo rake, and/or a wooden rake used for sand manipulation. As you use the wooden or bamboo rake to manipulate the sand, the tines on the rake create a wave like pattern in the sand representing water waves; this makes the garden an exceptional tool for meditations involving learning how to "go with the flow," or for trying to find solutions to overcoming obstacles in your day-to-day life.

Making it Magickal

You can add a bit of consecrated sea salt into the sand to ensure your sand garden maintains positive energy vibrations. You can also decorate the exterior of the garden with occult symbols.

Care, Maintenance, and Cautions

Keep your Zen Garden in a dry area. Keep animals and children away from your Zen Garden, and the accessories free from negative energies. Place the sand garden on a stable table or stand. Do not add too many objects to the design, as this will affect your ability to use the sand garden. If you get fresh sand from the beach, make sure it is free of critters or insects.

For the Crafty Witch

You can also make a Zen Garden from scratch by using a shoe box; cut down the box so that the sides are low, fill it with about an inch or two of sand, and add your ornamentations. You can also put sand into a low, rectangular plastic bowl. Add your favorite colored sand to your Zen Garden; there is nothing more striking than a Zen Garden made of rich purple, blue, or deep black sand. No matter what color sand you decide to use, you can add rainbow glitter to it; this is particularly beautiful if you use a sand garden with a tea light or votive candle or if you work with your Zen Garden out in the sunlight. You can add quartz crystals, small agate stones, or any kind of crystals you desire. You can also add shells. If you have a large garden, you can use a section to add a small Bonsai tree.

Trataka Stand

Description, Uses, and Symbolism

Trataka (pronounced *trah-tak-ah*) is the practice of staring into a flame or another object to improve one's ability to concentrate, focus, and to visualize. A Trataka stand is used to hold a candle; the stand is adjustable so that the flame of the candle is directly in front of the user's line of vision. The practice of Trataka is a yogic method of meditation, one used to gaze at a flame until it can be seen even when the eyes have been closed.

A Trataka stand is often made of steel; it can vary in terms of height, depending upon how the stand is adjusted. Usually the stand is about 13 centimeters to 80 centimeters high. The stand has an adjustable element that allows the user to pull on the upper portion of the stand so that its height can be extended. Later, when storing the stand, the user can push down on the top to return it to its original height. The Trataka Stand can hold candles that are one inch in thickness.

Trataka meditations help to improve focus and your visualization skills. After you have gazed at the flame and you have closed your eyes, turn your focus to the location of your third eye, positioned just above and between the brows. This type of meditation improves your third eye visualizations, and helps improve your ability to ignore environmental distractions during meditations, too.

Making it Magickal

Use a Trataka stand to hold a candle when fire scrying. To instill it with Magickal energies, cleanse, bless, consecrate, charge it, and use it during rituals or Magickal applications.

Care, Maintenance, and Cautions

Occasionally grease the adjustable components of the Trataka stand to keep the parts moveable. Use a bit of petroleum jelly on the tip of your finger and place it at each adjustable junction, or you can use a bit of bees wax to keep the parts from tightening or freezing. You will also have to remove the wax drippings from the stand to keep it looking attractive. To remove hardened wax, apply an ice cube to the wax accumulation for a few seconds: this will cause the wax to flake off with greater ease. Then simply use your fingernail to gently scrape off the wax. For excessive wax build up, put the stand in the freezer for a minute or two. Regularly clean your Trataka stand with an appropriate metal cleaner; however, make sure the stand is thoroughly cleaned, dried, and that there is no residue on the stand before using it again.

Make sure you place the stand on a solid, non-flammable surface. It should also be placed in a location where it will not be easily knocked over. Make any height adjustments to the stand before you light the candle, not after. If you light the candle and find that the height is incorrectly set, snuff the candle out before making height adjustments. Once you have established the correct height of the stand, then relight the candle flame.

If you are meditating on a candle flame, do not stare at the flame for extended periods or to the point that it causes you discomfort; instead, watch the flame for short periods and intermittently close your eyes to visualize the flame. If you find that gazing at the flame bothers your eyes, stop performing the meditation and try another technique. You should limit how often you practice this type of meditation to avoid damaging your eyes; you should only practice a few times a month, and for short sessions.

For the Crafty Witch

You can forgo the use of a Trataka stand and still gain the benefits of Trataka meditations. Use a tall candle holder or position a large pillar candle on an elevated surface that is set at eye level. Alternatively, you can meditate on a stone, a crystal, or an object of your choosing. As you meditate, gaze at the object until you are able to see the object clearly with your eyes closed.

If you decide to decorate the outside of the Trataka Stand with paints, glitter, or other decorative elements, make sure you do not use decorations that will hinder your ability to use the adjustable components of the stand. You can decorate the portion of the stand that holds the candle or you can decorate the base freely with gemstones, shells, or other ornamentations. You can also make special meditation candles or anoint your meditation candles to draw/repel specific energies as you meditate. Consider carving esoteric symbols into the candles you are using in the Trataka stand too.

The Self as Sacred Space

You may be surprised to discover that you are your primary Magickal tool; all Magick comes from within, and tools are only an extension of you. You move your will and intent through your tools, but your tools are never the source of your Magick. In fact, in the absence of all else, all you need is a healthy mind, body, and powerful intent to work Magick. Since Magick comes from within, you should treat your body as sacred space. Strive to live a healthy lifestyle, expand the mind through learning, and sanctify the body through self-purification before Magickal workings.

You can take a purify bath or a shower before ritual. When taking a bath, add purifying herbals to the bath water. If you choose to take a shower, you can visualize all the negativity attached to or within you flowing down the drain as you prepare your body for ritual. You can use the following Peace Bath ritual to ready yourself for Magickal endeavors.

Peace Bath / Ritual Bath

Take sea salt, 2 to 3 chamomile tea bags (strings removed), and fresh rose petals. Charge all of the latter ingredients for calming, tranquility, and peace. Draw a bath with water set at your desired temperature. You can create a tranquil setting by lighting candles and lavender incense. When your bath is nearly drawn, you can add sea salt, chamomile, and fresh rose petals to the water. Relax in the water as negative energies are cleansed away.

Magickal Hair Care

Your hair is an extension of your being and carries your essence. It should be guarded and treated with care and respect; many practitioners will keep their hair after it has been cut or trimmed. It can later be used in offerings or in spells. It can be fun and rewarding to bring your craft into the care of your hair, too. You can create essential oils or infusions to use as hair treatments by brewing an herb as a tea or adding slightly bruised or dried herbs to almond or olive oil. There are many all-natural, herbal solutions you can use to keep your hair in good condition.

Natural Hair Coloring

Henna is a safe and inexpensive alternative to hair dye. Henna leaves are ground, pounded, and sold in beauty and health food stores in powder form. Henna powder is an unappealing dull grey-greenish color, when mixed with hot water the henna turns a rich chocolate color. When applied to the hair it turns the hair color into rich red tones ranging from red or auburn to mahogany. The end resulting shade is highly dependent on the color of your hair before you color it.

Mixes found in stores often include ingredients that, while natural, produce a greater range of colors, from an orangey-red to dark red colors, while Henna only produces a range of red hues. Note that if you decide to use Henna for coloring your hair, the process can be quite messy, and henna coloring tends to fade faster than chemical hair coloring applications: this means you will have to repeat the coloring process more often, every few months or so. You can make the application of henna a sacred practice. If you turn your hair coloring session into a Magickal ritual, you can use your rite to transform yourself physically and to refresh yourself spiritually. When you color you hair, you will be using a completely natural method for doing so and the ritual can instill a sense of initiation. As you mix the henna powder with water the mixture turns into a mud-like substance; applying the substance to the hair allows you to make a deep connection with the Earth and the Goddess. Wait for the henna to set in forty to sixty minutes, depending upon the effect you desire. Use the waiting period to ground and center.

Witch Hazel

This is a powerful astringent for the skin, but it can also be used in hair for clarifying purposes. Use a spray bottle to apply it as a spritz in order to increase hair shine and curl.

Hair Sticks

One interesting way to use hair sticks is to rely on them as impromptu wands. You can charge the hair accessory with the intent of using it as a Magickal tool or charge the accessories with ritual energies by leaving them on the altar during ritual workings; then you can carry the Magickal energy with your throughout the day.

Rosemary Oil

Rosemary accentuates brown hair colors and strengthens all types of hair. It promotes hair and scalp health. This herb is associated with mental clarity and improved memory. When using an oil treatment for the hair, use it sparingly.

Aloe

The juice of the aloe plant can be used for treating damaged skin or hair. You can also use this healing herb as an all natural hair gel; you can get fresh gel by taking one or more plant leaves, slitting them down the length of the leaves, and taking the aloe fresh from the plant.

Plain Yogurt

While plain yogurt is not necessarily an herb, you can apply it to the hair in order to help remove the oils from oil treatments. Follow the plain yogurt application with a through rinsing with cool water to promote hair shine.

Neem

Neem is an herbal that has been used in Indian medicine practices for centuries, since it offers antimicrobial and antibacterial properties. When applied to the hair, it helps to make the hair soft, shiny, and strong. While the oil actually has a bitter smell, something comparable to garlic and rubber, the scent washes out with one shampoo. Neem works as a powerhouse for hair protection and nourishment. The oil is made from the seeds and leaves of the Neem plant and produces a scent that takes some getting used to, but the benefits are well worth it. You can apply Neem oil to the hair weekly. You should allow the oil to sit in the hair for about an hour before shampooing. Neem is an all natural insecticide; it can also be used to deal with dry scalp conditions, eczema, dandruff, and skin rashes as well. To treat the scalp, you can take a bit of the oil and gently massage it into your scalp. If you want to gain the advantages of using Neem without having to deal with the strong scent produced by Neem oil, you can get Neem in powder form, and mix it like you would mix henna before you apply it.

Rose Water

Rose water is available at most health food stores or you can make your own by adding fresh rose petals to consecrated water, heating the mixture, and allowing it to cool. Rose water can be used on the hair to add a fresh rose scent or it can be added to ritual bath water. Since the rose is a symbol of the Goddess, this water can help you establish a connection with the divine before Magickal workings. You can also use rose water, charged with a specific Magickal purpose, as a hair spritzer. You can add the water to a spray bottle and spray it on your hair every time you need a spiritual "pick me up."

Ritual Fasting

As long as you do not have a medical condition that prevents you from doing so, ritual fasting is recommended before ritual workings. Fasting helps to purify the body, and heightens your intuitive abilities. Some practitioners refrain from the consumption of meat for three or four days before a planned ritual as well; again this is done to increase one's psychic abilities. You should not, however, fast before performing defensive Magick, since you need to be well grounded when working Magickal applications for psychic/spiritual/physical defense.

When you consume food during ritual, it is often in the form of cakes and ales or when having libation. The libation should be blessed and consecrated before it is consumed. This will help you maintain a purified state. You can use the following consecration for libation. Following the consecration, we offer a simple meal blessing that you can use to bless every meal or to give gratitude for the blessings you receive. When you use the simple meal blessing, you will also ensure that you are only eating foods that contain untainted energies.

Consecration of Libation

Hold your projective hand over the food and drink for consumption. Say:

> Mother Earth I call to thee,
> To bless this food and drink with me,
> Through my hands and through our will
> Let only positive energy spill.
> Let them be purified with your light
> Let them be consecrated with your might,
> All negative influences now must flee,
> By our will, so mote it be.

Simple Meal Blessing

The following simple meal blessing can be used to bless food and drink following ritual practices or to bless your meals on a daily basis.

Fertile Lady of the Land, Great Goddess, Divine Earth Mother,
This food, a boon, eases and relieves both spiritual and bodily hunger,
This rune be spoken, upon this request,
Your favor bestowed, this meal is blessed.
(I/we) thank you for your daily gifts and for this drink and food,
By your bountiful gifts of plenty, (My/our) body, mind, and spirit (is/are) renewed.

Chapter 4

Divinatory Tools

"Travelers are fantasists, conjurers, seers—and what they finally discover is that every round object everywhere is a crystal ball: stone, teapot, the marvelous globe of the human eye."
—Cynthia Ozick

The Art of Divination

Divination is the practice of making predictions about the future. It is the art of discovering occult or hidden knowledge. The word divination comes from the Old French *divinité* meaning "to predict"; the modern French *divinité* meaning, "divinity," and the Greek word *dĭos* for "God;" when practicing divination, the messages you receive are therefore forms of communication with the Divine. While the term divination often conjures the notion of fortune-telling or foretelling the future, the definition is expanded to include the ability to see past and present events as well. As one example, when using Tarot cards, many layouts allow the card reader to examine the basis of a situation, and the recent past or past events that have brought about current conditions in relation to one's question.

Etiquette and Rules for Divinatory Practices

When you are readying yourself for divinatory practices, you will want to adhere to some basic etiquette:

You have to take care of any divinatory tools you choose to use; if the tools are to serve you well, they must maintain positive energies. Always remain aware of the influence of outside energies, both mundane and Magickal. You would not let someone wearing muddy shoes tromp through your home, all over your carpet, and jump up onto your brand new sofa. When it comes to tools for divination, your tools for divination are delicate, sacred, and should be treated as such.

Even with proper attention and care, you must be aware of the need to periodically cleanse, bless, consecrate, and charge the divinatory tools you use.

Stop believing in coincidence and start seeing things as synchronistic events. The old cliché "things happen for a reason," is true; the universe and everything in it are deeply interconnected. Remember, you will receive information on a "need to know" basis; you must be willing to pay attention to it when the information comes to you.

Universal messages and information can only be received from a mind that is clear, relaxed, and open. If you are focusing on the stressful issues happening to you each day, you will have considerable difficulty opening up to the universe and your subconscious so that you can receive psychic messages.

Don't confuse scrying with spying; the purposes for scrying are to find out necessary information, not to infringe on a person's privacy. Divinatory practices should only be conducted for the benefit of wisdom and growth.

When it comes to divination, if you do not really want the answer do not ask the question. Give serious consideration as to whether or not you really want a question answered before you ask it.

Resist the urge to use divinatory practices for spite or malice. Do not use the arts to obtain an unfair advantage over another or in a situation like gambling. Do not be surprised if you pay a karmic price if you use divination practices irresponsibly.

Resist the urge to feed the ego: do not offer psychic guidance for unethical questions, no matter how skilled you are or will appear to be.

Resist making inquiries into the death of yourself or another; consider the ramifications of such information. The answer is simple; everyone is going to die sometime, but asking questions related to the timing of a death has serious physical, emotional/psychological, and spiritual consequences. Think about it this way: what would you do with the information once you got it, except dwell on it?

Do not ever give medical advice when you are divining for someone else. You can suggest that a person get a physical soon or you can make a subtle suggestion that it may be time to pay attention to health matters, but do not offer medical advice.

Do not seek divinatory guidance repeatedly for the same inquiry within a short time span. Repetitiously asking the same question during divination will result either in the same answers you received in early sessions or in divinatory answers that are nonsense. If you start getting divinatory responses that make no sense whatsoever, it is an indication that perhaps the universe is tired of answering a question repeatedly, and that you are clearly not paying attention too! Pose a question, accept the answer, and wait for events to unfold before reposing the question. If you really do not like an answer you receive, consider what you can do to change the possible outcome. Remember, just because something is divined does not mean that the future is fixed; if you change your mind, change your actions, and look at situations with a new perspective, often times you can change the expected outcome. Once you have taken steps to alter a situation, you can return to divinatory methods to see if your new actions have made a difference in the predicted outcome.

Psychic Skill Enhancement

Start to look for symbols in everything around you; of course, this is not a cue for you to get overzealous and see omens in everything, rather, it is an exercise that can help increase your awareness of symbols. Look for icons, symbols in art, films, stories, and the like. Begin to acquaint yourself with the language of symbols. Create your own notebook of symbols for future reference. You will be amazed at how fun it can be finding symbols in advertising or art. Eventually you will begin to see the subtle messages that were intended by the artist or that are shaped by your own perceptions of the subject matter.

Begin to question the moment when you encounter symbols, especially if the symbols prove repetitive. In your mirror journal, note the times you see symbols, where you see them, and note the commonalities as well as the differences between symbols you encounter. Keeping notes on the symbols you come across will make it easier for you to identify repetitive appearances and developing patterns.

Engage in psychic training as if you have entered into psychic boot camp: daily or otherwise, the key to your success is found in regular practice of your skills. Learning to listen to your intuition takes time and practice. It can be especially difficult to listen to "gut feelings" if your hunches have been wrong in the past, or if you often ignore the messages given to you from your higher self.

Another exercise you can do is to try to discern who is calling you on the phone before you look at the caller ID or answer it. You might be surprised how often you are right. An alternative but similar exercise involves trying to discern which song will come on the radio before it is played; careful though, often times the radio show hosts give away the answer before a song comes on! You can also use things like horse races to see how intuitive you are; of course, we do not recommend gambling, but you can try to figure out what horse will come in and in what position in a specific race.

Of particular importance is noticing the hunches or gut feelings that seem to have come from nowhere at all; they appear quite suddenly. You may even find that the hunches you have do not always make sense to you. If you get this kind of a hunch, jot it down in your mirror journal so you can track its accuracy in the future. Try to make a note of the things that happened to you just before, during, and after you got the feeling or hunch too; this can help you identify triggers that kick start your intuitive abilities.

The Mind as a Divinatory Tool

The practitioner's mind is the ultimate dictionary of symbolism accessible for divinatory interpretations. When the mind is relaxed and attuned to guidance from the Divine, it will make all the difference between your ability to interpret messages using any elaborate system of divination and having attractive accessories that are unable to serve a purpose.

How you attune to your intuitive psychic nature depends on your preference, religious predilections, and personal style. No matter what methods you choose to attune yourself to universal energies there are key elements you need to adhere to during divinatory practices. First, you will want to make the practice of divination diligent; this means you should spend ample time meditating, using the divinatory tool you have chosen, and you will want to spend time documenting your experiences. You should document any premonitions, hunches, suspected omens, signs, dreams, synchronistic experiences, and repeating symbols or themes occurring in your day-to-day dealings.

Pay attention to colors, the repetitive or sudden appearance of animals, repetitious numbers, sudden or unexplained intuitions and sensations, inner voices, or unexpected insights and decisions you make. You also need to note the result or manifestation of the intuitive messages you receive. As you continue to increase your awareness and perception, you will be fine-tuning your receptive skills. Document success and failures as you practice divination: this will help you identify extra-sensory triggers and issues that might be preventing you from perceiving divinatory messages correctly.

Daily meditation is vital for anyone seeking to become adept in divination; meditative practices train your mind. Meditation also helps you achieve a state of awareness conducive for divinatory practices. Be consistent about your meditative practices, performing at the same time every single day whenever it is possible for you to do so. It is imperative that meditation practices become habitual: this can only be achieved through a regular routine. Use your meditation sessions as an opportunity to explore different meditative methods so you can identify what meditations appeal to you. You can try guided meditations if you are uncomfortable attempting the process on your own. Once you achieve greater skill during guided meditations, only then should you make an attempt at meditations without a guide.

Learning to ground, center, and clear away negative energies is an essential part of early psychic development and meditative work. You may want to put the following meditation on an audio tape so that it can serve as a guided meditation for you. You can also have another practitioner read the meditation aloud if you do not mind the presence of another person in the room as you meditate.

Psychic Development Meditation

You can use this meditation before you perform any divinatory applications. It will help ground and center you. It will also help open your third eye so that you can receive clear messages from the universe.

Find a comfortable chair to sit in or sit on the floor with your legs crossed. If you need back support, you can lean up against a sofa or soft chair. You should not lie down during your first attempts to meditate; you are likely to become too relaxed and drift into sleep. Your first few efforts at this meditation may prove a challenging process, but as you grow accustomed to it, you will find that the meditation flows with greater ease each time you use it.

Close your eyes and take five controlled breaths. When your breathing has slowed and your body relaxes, begin to feel the floor beneath your feet or where you are seated. Visualize and sense a streak of white energy flowing from your root chakra, located at the base of your spine, into the floor and down into the Earth: this is a grounding cord. The end of the grounding cord is what is anchoring you to the Earth.

As you remain anchored to the Earth, sense any negative residue or energies draining out of your body, through your root chakra, and down into the Earth via the grounding cord. You can even visualize this cord like a vacuum clearing out the negative residue in your body.

Once you feel freed from negative energy or residue, it is time to recharge. Feel and visualize powerful grounding energies from deep inside the earth as it rises through the earth, into the grounding cord, and into your body. This energy is revitalizing and it re-energizes you. Now visualize being able to see your own aura; the aura is clean, strong, and vibrant. Visualize a white bubble of light surrounding your aura, serving as protection from negativity. Make your intentions clear and use your will to allow only positive psychic messages to enter into the bubble, but disallow the entrance of negative energies or entities. The protective bubble you have created is both shield and filter.

Now systematically become aware of your chakras, one by one, beginning with the root chakra and moving up to the sacral, solar plexus, heart, throat, third eye, and crown chakra. See the chakras as vibrant, bright, colorful, and pure. Sense them as clear, in alignment and receptive.

Now sense the grounding cord extending from your root chakra into the earth, moving and extending up the center of your being. Allow the cord to move through each one of your chakras, out your head, and to extend into the vast universe. Let the cord connect you with the Divine Source of All. Note that the cord moves through you and is preparing you to receive information.

Next, in the location of your third eye, just between and above your brow, visualize the chakra opening. Here you will be able to see a blank television screen, movie screen, or window. Now remain open for message you will receive which will appear on the screen or window you are visualizing. Make note of any colors, symbols, or messages you receive; after the meditation you will need to document them.

When you feel you are done with this part of the meditation, you can leave the communication window or screen open/receptive to messages; you will fully remember any messages you have received during the meditation. To return to a normal state of consciousness, you can begin counting from one to twenty. With each number, you will become more conscious and aware of your surroundings. Upon reaching twenty, you can open your eyes, stretch, and enjoy the relaxed feeling you have that you can carry throughout the day.

Psychic Training

You can use very simple games to train your psychic mind and to learn how to trust your intuitive impressions. Perhaps as important as results is becoming familiar with how the feeling of guessing and intuition are different. As you learn how to identify intuitive impressions, you will gain greater confidence in your predictions, and when you learn to trust your psychic mind, it becomes more responsive to you by providing you with additional correct impressions. Bear in mind that the more you practice, the greater the likelihood that you will also quickly learn about psychic fatigue: a condition that occurs when your mind becomes overly tired, and you start receiving unclear, ambiguous, or flat out incorrect results. If you encounter psychic fatigue during your training, it is your mind's way of telling you it is time to take a break from your practice.

Picture This

You can use this psychic game to improve your ability to trust the messages you receive from your subconscious. This game can be played with one or more players. You can use random photographs, shuffle them, and place them face down on the floor. After all the photos have been positioned face down, choose one photo to work with; take up the photo in your receptive hand, without turning it over, and try to discern what the image is on the opposite side. Attempt to sense the scene, what is going on in the picture, the dominant colors, and the symbols or images in the photograph.

Jot down your impressions in a notebook. Make sure you do not dismiss any information just because your mind is telling you that the information is not valid or that it is incorrect. Simply be open to receiving the messages from your subconscious mind. This is very important and the information you get may not be wrong, merely a bit ambiguous. For instance, if you happen to sense or hear the ocean and you later flip over a picture you took when you went whale watching, you are noticing elements of the scene, even if they are not presenting you with the exact picture. When you have finished, you can flip the picture over and compare your notes with what is in the photograph.

Psychic Games with Playing Cards

There are some exercises you can perform to begin learning how to trust your intuition. Using an ordinary deck of cards, lay out cards face down and attempt to discern what is on the opposite side of each card. Beginners should start by only trying to figure out the color or suit of a card. Later, you can try determining the exact number on the card. You should keep track of your "hits" and "misses" every time you practice and pat yourself on the back when you notice improvements in your accuracy.

Basic Card Games

Shuffle the deck of playing cards and keep them face down on the table. Conduct the grounding/psychic preparation meditation offered in Chapter 3 of this book. Place one card face down with your receiving hand. Now visualize a blank screen and know that you will see the color of the card, either red or black, on the screen. Allow the color to appear slowly on the screen before you. Note your visions and compare with the card you have before you.

Move on to another card and repeat the process until you have worked your way through the deck. Make one pile for cards you have identified correctly and a separate pile for misidentifications. When you are finished, if you have determined a card's color more than twenty percent of the time, it illustrates that you are making determinations based on your intuition. Anything below twenty percent illustrates that you are only making guesses. Do this exercise on a regular basis so that you can strengthen your intuitive skills.

Once it becomes easy for you to identify the color of a card, change the game by attempting to visualize the color and suit of the card. Later, you can work toward trying to determine the color, the suit, and the number of each card you pull. You can perform this game alone or with others: Playing with others helps you to foster a friendly intuitive competition.

Who Has the Ace of Spades?

This psychic game is ideal for a group of players. Using a standard card deck, you can deal out five to seven cards to each player. Once the cards have been dealt, each player will attempt to sense who has the Ace of Spades in their hand or if the Ace of Spades is still in the deck. Each player should jot down their answer on a piece of paper so other players are not influenced by each other when responding. If you are the player that has the Ace of Spades in your hand, you can use visualization to attempt to block others from figuring out you have the card or you can use telepathy as you try to communicate to other players that you are the one holding the card in your hand. When everyone has noted their impressions, all players reveal their hands so that the winner can be determined.

The Psychic Shell Game

This game is suitable for two or more players. You will need several small shells, or similar small objects, and five to six boxes, containers, cups, or small envelopes. The goal of this game is to be able to conceal the objects or coins completely. Have one player conceal the selected objects in two or three out of the five or six containers. Now the second player can use visualization and/or psychometry to determine where the objects are hidden. To make the game more challenging, try to call out the object first before determining which container it is hidden in; like when a pool player announces which pocket the ball will go in, you are announcing where you will find a specific object in a specific container.

Coin Psychometry Game

This game is as easy as digging pocket change out of the couch cushions. Start with a pile of coins, large or small. Hold a single coin in your receptive hand. Visualize your psychic movie screen and allow your psychic mind to project onto the screen. Will your psychic mind to show you the date on the coin by presenting it onto the screen. Do not force an answer; wait patiently for the numbers to appear gradually on the screen before you. If you sense more than one date, try to feel which date is accurate. If you note other distracting information or unrelated information appearing on your visualized screen, will your mind to do away with the unnecessary information and to reveal only the details that you seek. Practice and record your results as you do so.

Psychic Experimentation

Consulting the Tarot can be a great way to build intuitive confidence. To strengthen both Tarot abilities and overall psychic confidence, try practicing readings for time limited results. For example, consulting a one- to three-card spread to ascertain pertinent messages for the day ahead gives you a short time frame that you can use to measure results. Bear in mind that many daily routines can be mundane or uneventful, so some relatively lackluster readings may ensue. You can use the cards in this way to gauge the potential conflicts you might face, what you will need to focus on, what the emotional theme of the day will be, or to anticipate potential surprises. Document the reading, your impressions, and how actual events compare to the reading. If you note any misinterpretations, this is an excellent time to learn from the experience as well. If you want to put a different spin on your experiments, try to conduct small readings regarding the upcoming news headlines or use other measurable outcomes. Just make sure you use brief time frames so that you can easily compare your divinatory practices with real-world outcomes efficiently.

Many books instruct you to meditate on a Tarot card when you draw it so that you can begin to understand some of the symbols on the card. It is even better if you take the time to examine all of the cards in the deck thoroughly before you begin to use them. Use a notebook and make a single page for every card in the deck you have chosen. Using a magnifying glass, take a very close look at each card and note the things you see. Make notes on the colors, images, and the actions depicted in the card. Make notes on the background of the images too. As you document what you see, ask yourself what season is represented; what astrological symbols are on the cards; what numerological information is on the cards, and what major archetypes the cards depict.

Divinatory Methods

Divination has been practiced for centuries: The Ancient Babylonians, Egyptians, Chinese, Japanese, Greeks, and Romans all practiced the art of *oneiromancy* or dream interpretation, just one form of many divinatory techniques. An array of tools can be used for modern divination practices, depending upon the type of divinatory practice you choose. Here we explore just some of the countless tools you can use for divination.

Pendulum

Description, Uses, and Symbolism

The term pendulum comes from the Latin word *pendulus,* meaning "to suspend or hang."[12] Using a pendulum for divination purposes is called *dactylomancy*. A pendulum is a small weighted object attached to a chain or string. The weighted object can be made of stone, crystal, a pendant, a needle, or another object that is heavy enough to force the string or chain to hang still and straight. Some pendulums have a small piece on the upper portion of the chain to make them easier to hold between the index finger and the middle finger. Some pendulum users like clasping the pendulum between their index finger and thumb.

The pendulum can be used for spirit communication and it can be used for requesting answers to "yes" and "no" questions. If you do not have a pendulum board, simply determine what directions are indicative of yes or no responses; for instance, if the pendulum swings forward and back or up and down, this can indicate a "yes" response; if the pendulum swings from left to right or vice versa, this can be indicative of a "no" response.

Making it Magickal

You can use pendulums for self-hypnosis, the hypnosis of others, and to invoke a trance-like state, although this is easier if one person is manipulating the pendulum swing while another concentrates on the swinging weight. Like dowsing rods, you can use pendulums for locating specific energies during healing sessions, when looking for energy imbalances, or attempting to find lost items. Some practitioners even use a pendulum to detect positive and negative energies: When the tool swings clockwise, or deosil, the energies are positive, but when the tool swings counterclockwise, or widdershins, the tool is detecting negative energies. The swinging of the pendulum in a deosil or widdershins direction can also be indicative of "yes" and "no" responses, or when healing, deosil and widdershins can be indicative of open and blocked energy channels or meridians respectively. Sometimes, the pendulum will literally "pull" forward, to the left or to the right. This may be indicative of a nearby body of water or it can also indicate the presence of a spirit. Cleanse, bless, consecrate, and charge your pendulum before use.

Care, Maintenance, and Cautions

Always remember that your own movement must not influence the pendulum when you use it to avoid incorrect responses: this is where the hard part comes into play! It is a lot more difficult to stand perfectly still or to keep your arm from moving and affecting the swing or direction of the pendulum than you might first imagine. In fact, you should take considerable time just practicing the art of holding the pendulum still. You can start out by resting your elbow on a flat surface, so that you can steady your hand while using the pendulum until you get better at holding your outstretched arm perfectly still.

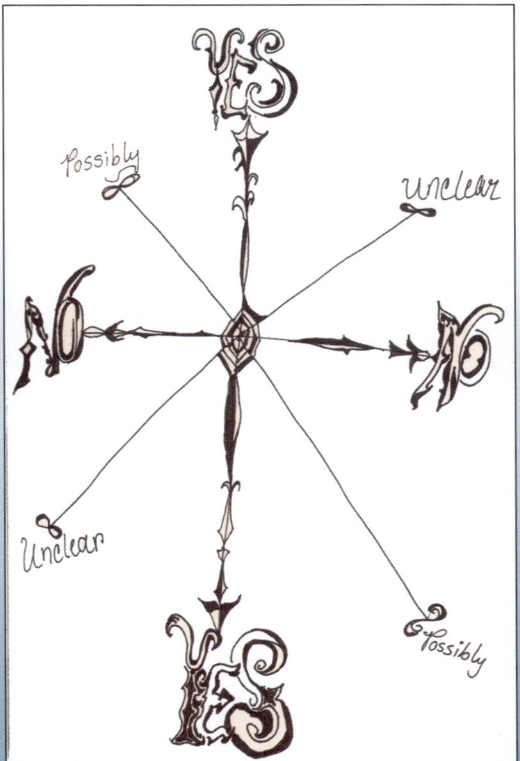

Pendulums are used for divination and spirit communication. Here is an example of how you can make or decorate your own pendulum board on the left and a simple pendulum board design on the right.
Illustration by Angela Kaufman; graphic by Dayna Winters.

For the Crafty Witch

You can use a piece of jewelry, like a pendant and chain as a pendulum if you do not happen to have a pendulum on hand. You can also use an old key, a ring, or you can string a series of different crystals conducive to divination on some fishing line and make your own hand-made pendulum. If you do not have a pendulum board, you can create one using a large piece of paper or cardboard; your pendulum board can be as elaborate as you like, and you can even create one made out of a flat piece of wood.

Scrying

Scrying is the art of interpreting symbols as they emerge in a liquid, fire, smoke, or as seen in or on a medium with a reflective surface. The meaning ascribed to the symbols can be both cultural and personal. Practice is essential in order to recognize emerging symbols. You will also need to develop your symbolic understandings so that you can easily interpret the meanings the images hold for you. Before any scrying session, you will want to meditate; this relaxes the body and helps you ready the mind for the task. You will need to be grounded before you begin the scrying process. You can use the following spell to enhance your scrying practices.

Scrying Spell

Light a purple candle, since purple is associated with the third eye and psychic visions. You can use an array of psychic enhancing incense including things like cinnamon, lotus, rose, or frankincense. After lighting the candle and incense, say:

The veil concealing the beyond lifts for me,
Images arise in the (smoke, water, fire, crystal ball, etc.) of what will be,
As I watch, truth unfolds,
Past and future now foretold.

Crystal Ball

Description, Uses, and Symbolism

There are many forms of scrying, the most popular being the use of a crystal ball. If you decide to get a crystal ball, you will need to prepare the ball for use. The crystal ball needs to be blessed, consecrated, and charged. Charge the ball by the light of the full moon by leaving the ball stand for three consecutive nights. Keep the ball safe when it is not in use. Your crystal ball needs to be kept out of the sunlight when you are not using it. You should wrap it in a soft black cloth when you store it to keep negative energies from affecting the ball.

Making it Magickal

You can charge your crystal ball by moonlight by leaving it by the window in the evening when the moon is full. Cleanse, bless, consecrate, and charge the ball before using it. Periodically re-cleanse and recharge the ball as necessary.

Care, Maintenance, and Cautions

Never leave your crystal ball in sunlight; this diminishes the energies of the ball. If you are going to wash the ball, you can do so with a mixture of mugwort and cold water. Mugwort is a great herb for visions and the cold water will not leave a residue on the ball. Keep the ball covered in a black cloth whenever it is not in use.

For the Crafty Witch

If you are on a tight budget, you can use a witch's gazing ball made of hand blown glass instead of a crystal ball for scrying. If you are interested in antique tools, there are also antique witch's gazing balls you can invest in to use for scrying purposes. Modern gazing balls are sometimes less expensive than crystal balls, and they are made of things like glass, stainless steel, or chrome. Alternatively, you can use other inexpensive scrying methods too, like mirrors, water, or scrying with flame. If you desire, you can make a decorative pillar stand or a handmade ball holder for the scrying object you choose.

Mirrors

Description, Uses, and Symbolism

An ordinary mirror can be converted into a Magick mirror for the purposes of scrying; the user gazes upon the surface of the mirror until images form upon the surface or in the mind's eye. You can also buy a Magick mirror online. It can take you several sessions before you get any results from a Magick mirror. You may want to document your sessions so you can keep track of your visions.

Making it Magickal

You can use a mugwort wash to enhance the properties of the mirror, and you should cleanse, bless, consecrate, and charge it when the moon is full. Smudge the mirror every other month or whenever you feel its positive energies waning. Anoint your third eye with a bit of mugwort diluted in consecrated water to improve your psychic abilities.

Care, Maintenance, and Cautions

You should keep the surface of the scrying mirror perfectly clean. Make sure you do not accidently drop the mirror. If you break the mirror, discard it by burying it. Since mirror scrying is also a form of spirit communication, you should seal the mirror by using consecrated water and your finger to mark it with a pentacle before using it. Visualize the pentacle being created out of a blazing blue fire as you create the mirror's Magickal seal. Wrap the mirror in black material to keep it free of negative energies.

For the Crafty Witch

You can make a Magick mirror out of a cut piece of glass; a black backing is applied to the mirror so that you can scry more readily into the surface of the glass. If you have a piece of glass and you do not have a black backing, you can use spray paint or regular black paint to color one side of the glass. You also have the option of converting a small mirror into a scrying device; you can decorate the device any way you choose, just make sure the embellishments do not make it difficult to scry into the glass's surface. You can use the following spell to enhance your crystal ball or Magick mirror before use.

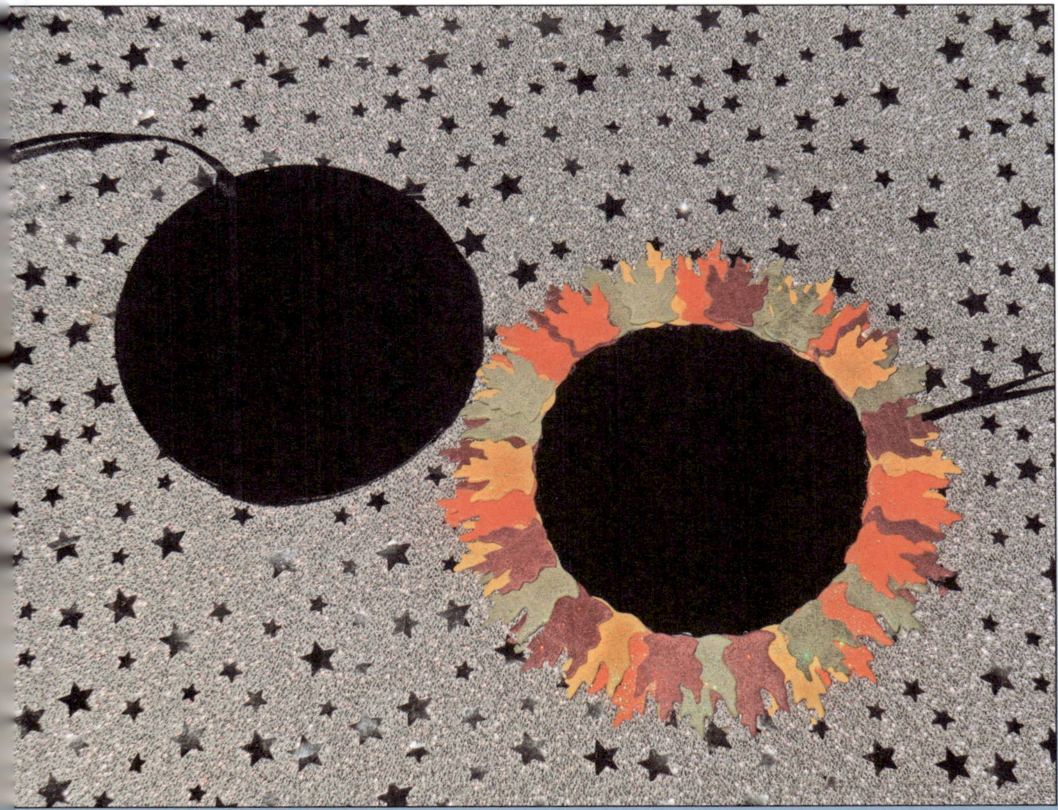

Magick Mirror and Crystal Ball Preparation

Burn mugwort incense or another incense aligned with psychic workings. Say the following:

Silver mirror/crystal ball, on this night,
Open the gates to unlimited sight,
That which I request to know,
Your surface now will show.
You reflect what I need to see,
Revealing the past, present, and what is to be.
Bring to me an image here,
Sights unseen are now made clear.

Runes

Description, Uses, and Symbolism

As mentioned earlier, the term *rune* comes from the Gothio word *runa*, meaning "line, furrow, and mystery," and the Middle English word *rún,* meaning "counsel"; the term signifies letters or runic characters etched in stone.[13] Runes are not only an ancient form of writing, in ancient cultures the writing was an art form only known to a select few, like scribes; thus the act of writing was secretive and mysterious.[14] Runes are not only a Magickal form of writing, but they are also used to forecast future events or to find out the answers to "yes/no" questions.

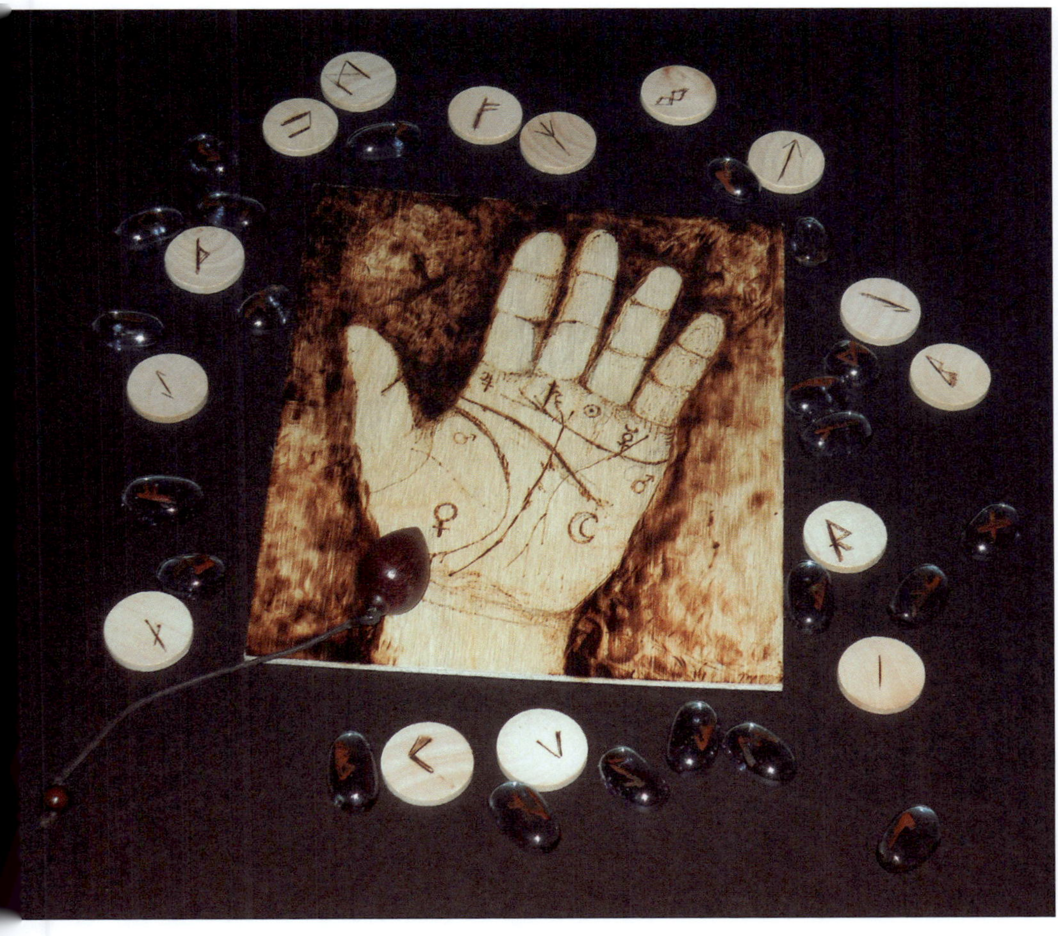

When you use runes, you will need a bag for storing them. Runes are used much like Tarot cards, where you have to concentrate on a question or situation as you draw the runes from the bag. There are many different layouts you can use when casting stones as well. You can choose one stone or several. One of the best ways to determine if you have a drawn enough stones is to sense whether or not you are done with the casting intuitively.

Making it Magickal

Cleanse, bless, and consecrate the stones before use. Periodically smudge the stones with sage to ensure their energies remain positive.

Care, Maintenance, and Cautions

When you draw runes, pay attention to the way you pull them out of the bag. Some stones have reversed meanings. Like Tarot cards, you should keep your rune stones out of the hands of others that may transfer negative energies. Remember, any future event that you divine with runes is not definite and that things can be changed depending upon the actions you take.

For the Crafty Witch

When you buy a set of runes it usually comes with a small guide for interpreting the stones. If you decide to make your own runes, you can get interpretative meanings online or from various books on the subject of rune casting. You can use regular rocks that you gather from outdoors, tumbled stones, or you can even use crystals or pieces of round wood to make your own runes. Look for stones that have a relatively flat surface so it is easier for you to add each rune depiction. If you choose wood materials, you can burn or carve the runes into each. Otherwise, you can paint runes onto the stones you choose. If you desire, you can also make a special bag for your runes out of black material, or make a rune cloth to lay stones upon during divinatory sessions, as well as storing the stones when not in use.

Tarot

Description, Uses, and Symbolism

The practice of using Tarot cards or playing cards for divinatory purposes has an ambiguous history; there are works of art that depict the King of Spain working with a fortune teller who is using cards to determine the future.[15] Some attribute the birth of the Tarot card game to Renaissance, Italy. The Tarot is a deck of 78 cards, consisting of 22 Major Arcana cards numbered 0 to 21, and 56 Minor Arcana cards consisting of different suits like wands, cups, pentacles, and swords. Each card suit is associated with an element; wands are associated with air (some practitioners associate the wands with fire), pentacles are earth, swords are associated with fire (some practitioners associate swords with air), and cups are associated with the element of water. Each suit consists of the following cards: the Ace, Knight, Queen, King, (some decks have Pages), and numbered cards from two to ten. When you are divining with cards, like the Tarot for example, you are engaging in cartomancy or chartomancy.

Tarot predicts conditions and emergent patterns of events, personalities, or both. It is less devised for "yes" or "no" questions and proves better for open-ended questions or guidance. Tarot cards can be used to gain insight or guidance in a situation, and can be used for meditation purposes or as a storyboard to develop writing ideas. Carl Jung's followers also relied on the Tarot as a method of self-discovery in therapy sessions.

To perform a reading you will need to focus on the situation or question you have as you shuffle the entire deck. Some Tarot users continue to shuffle the deck until the deck reveals a "leaper": a card that seemingly jumps out of the deck. You have the option of including the leaper in the reading or setting it aside before you begin placing cards in any layout you choose. The meanings of spreads vary from one interpreter to another: for instance, when laying out three cards each card might be indicative of events occurring in the next three days or the next three weeks. The cards can also be read as past, present future, or choices A, B, and C.

Making it Magickal

Whether you buy a deck of Tarot cards or they are gifted to you, you need to consecrate them before use. You will also have to charge the cards with your personal energies; this can be done by placing the cards under your pillow at night while you sleep for a period of three nights.

Care, Maintenance and Cautions

You will want to repeat the recharging process, whenever you feel the energies of the cards have changed or are dissipating. If you begin doing readings and find that the answers are nonsensical or repeatedly do not apply to your situation or question, it is indicative that your cards are in need of a recharge. Always remember that the divinatory responses you get from Tarot cards are actually possibilities, all of which can be influenced by the actions you take in the present and near future. Consider the ethical guidelines offered in the beginning of this chapter whenever you offer Tarot readings to another individual.

For the Crafty Witch

If you do not have a deck of Tarot cards or another type of oracle deck, you can use traditional playing cards consisting of fifty-two cards whenever you want to divine something. When using playing cards for divination, the black cards indicate struggles or omens; the red cards are indicative of opportunities or a time of high energy. Each card suit, like the tarot, is associated with an element and a theme. The hearts are cards representing emotional or social endeavors, thereby making them associated with the element of water. Diamonds are associated with goods, money, and work or tangible objects; thus, the cards are associated with earth. Spades represent strife, obstacles, or challenges, are associated with fire. Clubs are associated with inspiration, communication, new beginnings, and opportunities, so they are also associated with the element of air. The face cards in the deck are representative of people; the kings represent adult or mature males, the queens adult or mature females, and the Jack can be indicative of young men or women. Aces are cards representing new beginnings and/or specific seasons. You can find an array of playing card meanings online for the purposes of divination.

Dowsing Rods

Description, Uses, and Symbolism

Water divination is referred to as hydromancy, and one of the most common forms of this type of divination is the use of dowsing rods. Dowsing Rods come in two forms; Y-shaped rods made from a branch that naturally forms a Y-shaped fork at the end of the branch or contemporary rods made of metal. The newer rods used by diviners have an L-shaped design, with the short end of the rod serving as the handle. Dowsing rods have been successfully used for finding underground sources of water, but they are also used to detect disturbances in the electromagnetic field. Dowsing rods are also sometimes relied on by practitioners of the healing arts to discover auric blockages.

If you buy dowsing rods from a store, they are sold in pairs. You can hold one dowsing rod in each hand, but the goal is to hold the rods loosely so that you are not manipulating the dowsing rods as you hold them. The long end of the rods should be facing in front of you and allowed to move by themselves in whatever direction the rods are "pulled."

Making it Magickal

Whether you buy or make your dowsing rods, make sure you cleanse, bless, consecrate, and charge them. If you use the rods during spirit communication sessions or when attempting to detect spirit activity, make sure you re-cleanse the rods to keep them free of negativity.

Care, Maintenance, and Cautions

Keep the rods wrapped in a black cloth to keep negative energies out and positive energies in the rods. Do not let others meddle with the tools or play with them; this can transfer negative vibrations to the tool.

For the Crafty Witch

You can use coat hangers or thin rods of metal to make your own dowsing rods; you will need a pair of pliers so that you can bend the rods at the ends to make handles. For added flexibility during movement, you can add straws to the handles so the rods can freely move in your hands when in use.

Astrology

Description, Uses, and Symbolism

Astrology is the practice of using the stars, constellations, and planetary alignments to predict or foretell future events as well as to determine the specific life path and personality traits of an individual. The term Astrology is derived from the Latin and Greek word *astrologia* meaning "knowledge of the stars."[16] The term *astrologia* at one time encompassed the art of astrology as well as the astronomy, the scientific study of the stars.[17] Later, a division between the two practices was created, as is reflected by the two separate terms in use today; the separation was due to views of astrology as pseudoscience versus astronomy being viewed as a legitimate field of scientific inquiry.[18] Today, astrological charts can tell you a lot about yourself or another individual, and there are myriad methods for getting an astrological chart. If you plan to learn astrology, you will need an ephemeris (a table of planetary movements), a compass, writing implements for documenting charts and forecasts, and accurate birth date, time, and location information.

Making it Magickal

Some witches like to choose a specialty and you may find that you have an affinity for astrology. If you are so inclined, the use of astrology and astrological forecasting can become a part of your lifelong, Magickal journey. You may also only decide to have readings done once a year, before esbats, sabbats, or special power days. You also have the option of planning daily or Magickal endeavors based upon planetary influences and/or planetary hours.

Care, Maintenance, and Cautions

While there is not any physical care involved in using astrology, other than concern for the condition of your books and resources, you still have a few cautions to consider. First, do not assume that the horoscope you get in the daily newspaper is accurate because usually it is so generalized that the prediction is really a hit or miss. That is because newspaper horoscopes are not individualized; they are based on Sun signs only. Learning astrology is a lengthy process; you may choose to go to someone that offers astrology readings. If you do, make sure you assess the reputation of the individual and find out how much experience they have before you rely on them to offer you astrological information. You should undergo at least a year of study in astrology before you begin reading charts for others; this will allow you to become fluent in the practice as well as a more confident astrologer.

For the Crafty Witch

If you are so inclined, you can map out your own astrological charts. You can also purchase software that will generate complex charts for you. You might want to consider keeping extensive notes on the predictions you make so that you can track the accuracy of your forecasts.

Bibliomancy / Stichomancy

Description, Uses, and Symbolism

Stichomancy is a divination practice involving the use of books, particularly those that contain poetry. The term *stichomancy* is derived from the Greek words *stichos* and *manteia*; *stichos* meaning "lines or verses," and *manteia* meaning, "divination or prophecy."[19] Likewise, the term *bibliomancy* comes from a combination of the Greek words *biblion* and *manteia*, with *biblion* meaning books.[20] Bibliomancy at one time referenced using the bible to retrieve random verses for the purposes of divination, but the term has since expanded to mean the use of any kind of book for fortune telling purposes. Books filled with poetry serve as excellent resources for practices involving stichomancy since poetic verses are short passages jam packed with images and connotations, all of which can be interpreted different ways by different people.

Making it Magickal

Some people use the I Ching for stichomancy practices or various religious texts, but you can choose a book that appeals to you at the immediate moment as well, thereby giving credence to the notion that nothing is coincidental and that the book is appealing to you at the specific moment in time for a specific reason. You can also consider using Magickal texts or Magickal reference books; for example, if you are having an issue at work with unsavory energies, you can perform stichomancy with a reference book on crystals or herbs; you will be surprised by what the random selections offer you in the way of potential information, insights, or solutions.

Pose a question and pick up any random book, flip through its pages, and choose a random passage to interpret in relation to your question. You can do variations on stichomancy readings, just as you can with Tarot cards. You can select a single verse to get a general answer to your query or you can choose three verses from the same book or different books, each verse representing the past, present, or future. You can also choose four verses corresponding to each of the four elements: Air, Fire, Water, and Earth. The passage you choose for the air element represents communications or things you need to be conscious of; the passage for the fire element can represent the actions you need to take in a situation. The passage for the water element can represent your emotional outlook, and the final passage for the earth element can represent upcoming events or changes in the mundane world in relation to your question.

Care, Maintenance, and Cautions

What is great about stichomancy is that the only thing you have to maintain and care for when doing these types of reading is your books or the material you are using for divination. However, over the long term, you might want to take notes on the passages you retrieve for interpretation. This will allow you to think about their meaning, perhaps write out interpretations, and allow you to check the accuracy of the readings over time. The art of stichomancy is easy to practice, but some verses are not always necessarily easy to interpret. Sometimes, when you perform a reading the passage will not make any sense to you at all. If the passage does not seem to fit your question or situation, it applies to another situation that your mind is wrestling with at the time you conduct the reading. It can also mean the events divined have not yet occurred and therefore are proving unclear to you, or you are missing the metaphorical value of the passage you are interpreting.

For the Crafty Witch

If you do not have any books handy, but you have online access, you can perform a basic stichomancy reading online. You can also try stichomancy readings by using magazines or newspapers as well. If you enjoy the art of writing or if you journal a lot, you might enjoy using your own writings for the purposes of stichomancy. Taking old journals and using some of the passages for a reading may lead you to some very personalized insights concerning your questions.

Palmistry

Description, Uses, and Symbolism

The term palmistry is derived from the Latin word *palma,* meaning "hand"; this divinatory art, also known as chiromancy,[21] involves divining the future or determining a person's personality traits through the examination of the lines on the palm, wrists, and fingers. There are two distinct forms of palmistry. Chiromancy, which involves the examination of the individual lines, marking, and mounts on each hand, and chirognomy, the act of deriving interpretations from examining the shape of the hands, of the fingers and nails, and the length of the fingers.

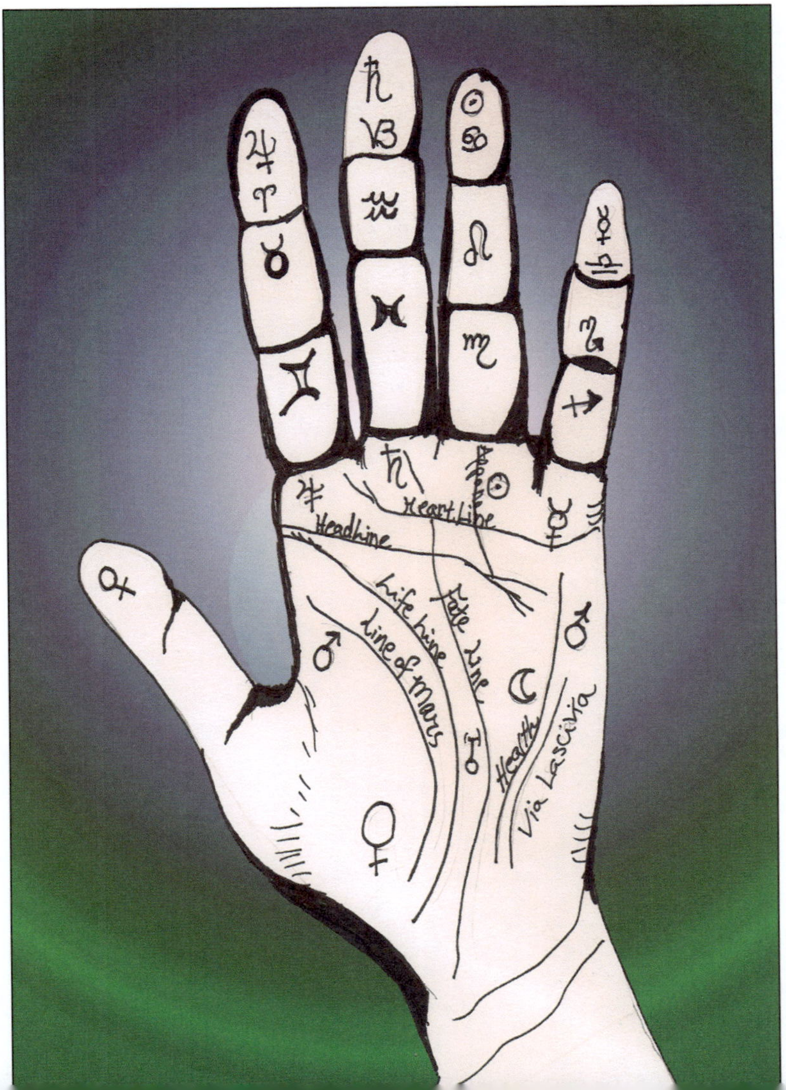

Making it Magickal

If you want to have a more intuitive palmistry session, you should meditate before you begin the palm reading. You can burn incense that will heighten your psychic senses and your intuitive awareness before you begin. You might want to invest in one or more palmistry resources, but you can find some information on interpretations online as well.

Care, Maintenance, and Cautions

Always remember that just because a line on your hand indicates a potential future, it is only a possible future and it is not set in stone. In fact, as one ages, the lines on the hands can change significantly.

For the Crafty Witch

If you are so inclined, you can draw a map of your own hands so that they are easier to assess. The act of drawing something causes you to pay attention to the finer details of what you are drawing. You can add your palmistry discoveries to your mirror journal too. You can also practice your palmistry skills on loved ones so you can grow more confident in your ability to interpret the lines and shapes of the hands.

Divination Methods Not Recommended

There are a number of divinatory practices performed in ancient times that are not recommended forms of divination today. For example, in some ancient cultures people performed divination by using animal sacrifices; this is seriously frowned upon today and it is not even necessary, since there are many other forms of divination you can use.

Some people divine by using the Ouija Board, and this is also not a recommended practice. While some people will argue that there is absolutely no danger in using an Ouija Board, others will firmly argue that there are myriad psychological and spiritual dangers that one faces when using the board for spirit communication or divination. The Ouija's use may draw negative energies or entities to you, or it can be the catalyst for spiritual attachments or attacks. Since the use and safety of the Ouija is highly debated, it is best to refrain from its use as a divinatory or spiritual communication tool.

Chapter 5
Establishing Sacred Space

The Magickal Use of Color in the Home

"Witchery is merely a word for what we are all capable of."
—Charles de Lint

Establishing sacred space is more than just constructing a Magick circle. You face several considerations when you choose the location of your sacred space, and how you establish it. Sometimes you have to negotiate areas of the home that you can dedicate to your Magickal workings: this is particularly true if you are living with others. In addition, once you have the free space to use, you will want to consider the existing décor and how you stage the area. Always remember that as you are establishing your sacred area, the intent behind every action is what will make the location and its contents sacred.

When decorating your Magickal abode, give serious consideration to the energies that every color has; colors have a powerful effect on your mood, thoughts, and health. If you choose the right colors for your furnishings and accessories, you can infuse a room with the vibratory energies of colors so that you can manifest specific results. Following, you will find what each color vibration offers and the Magickal correspondences of each.

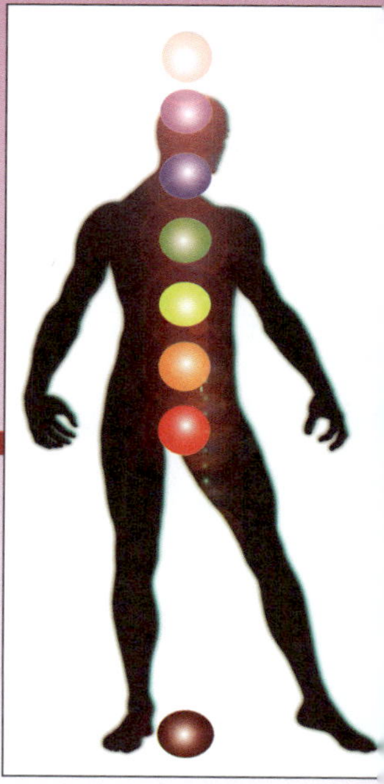

Red

Red is a color associated with potency, lust, aggression, passion, motivation, power, strength, the life force, anger, and the Fire element. Red is associated with the root chakra, so it is also a color linked to self-confidence, survival, sexuality, courage, vigor, and self-esteem. You can use red as an accent color in your home. An accent wall in the bedroom or in your dining room, since red stimulates to physical/sexual appetites. You can use red on your altar, but you will want to be moderate about the color's use; too much red can prove over-stimulating or it can alter your mood in a negative way. Pink is a milder form of red, so if you want to incorporate a lot of red in a room, it is better to use colors like magenta or pastel pink. Pink is associated with compassion, love, nurturing, the feminine, and tenderness; thus, this color is ideal for a child's bedroom or a master bedroom.

Orange

Orange is a mixture of yellow and red and therefore carries the subtle energies of both colors. Orange is a color used in Magickal applications when a person wants to attract something to them; this color should be used in moderation since you do not want to attract more energies than needed. Orange, like red, stimulates the appetite, so it may not be the best color for dining rooms or a kitchen where a person is attempting to limit their eating habits. If you choose to use this color in the dining room, you can use it as a color for trim or for an accent wall, to keep the appetite stimulating properties subdued. This color is associated with the element of fire, with autumnal ceremonies and celebrations, and it is symbolic of success, stimulation (both mental and physical), and the act of overcoming obstacles. Orange is associated with the sacral or second chakra and is therefore representative of energy, respect (both of self and others), and confidence.

Yellow

Yellow is associated with Air and Fire elements; thus, this color has solar symbolism. Yellow is associated with communication, memory, vitality, mental clarity, psychic abilities, confidence, and creativity. Yellow is associated with the third chakra or the solar plexus; it is therefore associated with alertness, intelligence, and wisdom. Yellow is an excellent color to accentuate your sacred space, but you do not want to overdo it. A moderate amount of yellow can elevate the mood, but too much yellow can cause anxiety. Yellow is good for a study, since it stimulates memory, or if it is used sparingly in a child's bedroom, as well as in a home office or den. Since yellow is symbolic of joy, it is also a good color to use in a kitchen. If you like a coppery yellow or gold colors, this type of yellow is great for a home office or library; it is associated with success, and gold is specifically associated with solar or God energies. It is also a color associated with love, as well as passion, so copper makes a nice accent in a bedroom, too.

Green

Green is associated with the element of Earth. This color's Magickal correspondence is fertility, abundance, growth, healing, nurturing, love, compassion, motherly energies, and the Divine feminine. This color is associated with the fourth chakra or the heart chakra; thus, is associated with love of the self and emotional as well as physical balance. Green is excellent if you want to remain grounded in your workings. It is also fantastic for your living room, where it conjures peace, compassion, nurturing, and harmony. You can also use green in a bedroom or den if you are looking to instill nurturing and harmonious energies.

Blue

Blue is associated with the element of water; its Magickal correspondences are emotions, the subconscious, dreams, the Divine feminine, healing, psychic abilities, and cleansing. Blue is associated with the throat chakra or fifth chakra, and is therefore associated with wisdom and decision making tasks. A dark blue is ideal for a bedroom if you want a tranquil environment conducive to dreaming. A light blue, such as turquoise, is associated with protection so it is a good color in any room. Various shades of blue are good for a work environment as well or in any location where you are constantly making weighty decisions. If you want an area in the home that induces a sense of tranquility and calming, you can accentuate the room with blue trim, blue border, or a blue accent wall.

Indigo

Indigo is a mixture of blue and purple, so it carries the subtle energies of both; this color is associated with Akasha or the combination of all the elements. It is also associated with the sixth chakra or the third eye. This color's Magickal correspondences include psychic abilities, the subconscious and conscious mind, and connecting to the divine. It also represents calming and tranquility or the ability to calm the mind, thus making it a superb color for a meditation area or your altar room. You can add this color to your bedroom if you want to have more psychic dreams. If you do not want to paint your entire altar area indigo, you can simply use indigo in the doorway or entrance so that upon entering, your conscious mind is calmed and the psychic mind is stimulated.

Violet

Violet is a color associated with Akasha and its Magickal correspondences include mysticism, the subconscious mind, the gateway of communication between the self and the higher self, and divine communication. Violet is associated with the crown chakra, and is connected to psychic abilities, royalty, knowledge of the self, and power. Violet is a mixture of blue and red so it can carry the subtle energies of each. Like indigo, this color is excellent for increasing psychic abilities and calming the mind, thereby making it a good color for meditation areas, bedrooms, altar rooms, or for room accents like pillows, and throws.

White

White is associated with the East, and is a symbol of new beginnings, communication, purity, innocence, exorcism, divination, protection, and divine communication. White is associated with the Soul Star chakra just above the head. As mentioned previously, white is both the inclusion of all colors (as a sound wave) and the exclusion of all colors (as a light wave), making it a suitable color to replace any other color in the spectrum. You can use white in any room to elevate the vibration of a room, and to give the room a clean, pure vibration. Interestingly, when adding white to any other color, it diminishes the color's Magickal properties. If you would prefer an accent that is a bit cooler and more striking than white, you can opt for silver accents in a room; silver is associated with feminine energies, the moon, the Feminine Divine, healing, intuition, psychic senses, and the mysteries.

Black

Black is a color associated with the North and Earth. Its Magickal correspondence includes protection, repelling, healing, and balancing. It is also associated with the Earth Star chakra just below the feet. This color is great for grounding, but you want to use it in moderation, since it can spark a depressive mood. As mentioned earlier, black is a mixture of every color. It is excellent as an accentuating color in an altar room, meditation area, or in a bedroom. Grey is black subdued by the color white, so it carries the diminished properties of both white and black. Interestingly, adding the color black to any color intensifies its properties.

Brown

Brown is associated with the North and the element of Earth. This color is ideal for use when healing animals. The color is ideal for a room where you want to invoke a sense of stability or if you want to emphasize grounding. It is a great color forf a home office, library, or study area, since the color is associated with centering and focusing. Brown is a mixture of orange and green, so its mild attractant properties and equally mild grounding properties make it a perfect color for a kitchen or a dining area. Brown incites a sense of nurturing, so it is good in the living room too.

Porches, Balconies, Entryways, Doorways, and Windows

Enclosed or open, wraparound or small balcony, a porch declares the entry space between the outside world and your home or your sacred space. These areas are what stand between the distractions from the outside world and the peace and tranquility generated inside the home. Porches, balconies, entryways, doorways and even windows serve as a midpoint or a "between space," not at all unlike the space or veil separating the realm of Magick and the mundane world. That being the case, you will want to have protective elements in these areas to help keep negative energies from passing through the entry, beyond the threshold of the between space and into your tranquil domain. These areas can ideally be decorated with statues of guardians, totems, chimes, and other protective symbols to keep negative energy at bay.

Bear in mind that as you enter your home you should begin to make it a habit of casting aside any of the negative energies that you have accumulated while you were outside of your domain. The notion of leaving "work at work" applies here; of course, leaving any emotions or work stresses at work is not as easy as you might think, and this is particularly true if you work at home in the first place. If you work outside the home, you should definitely start practicing the act of leaving your negative emotions and stressors outside the door. In fact, if you have a door mat outside the front door, visualize all of your negative emotions flowing down your body and out your feet. As you wipe your feet on the mat, visualize yourself freeing yourself from any negativity. Take a few deep cleansing breaths, and then cross over the threshold into your home.

If you actually work at home, try designating a small space to your work area if you do not already have an office space. It is a bit harder not to let your work environment creep into your living space/environment when you work in the home, but with a bit of practice and persistence, you can keep work stressors/emotions confined to separate spaces or areas in your home environment. You can also try taking a shower after work to cleanse away negative energies, visualizing the negativity flowing out of your body and down the drain as you do so. Quickly washing the hands under cold water and shaking them can also assist you in alleviating negative energies as well. You might want to consider regularly smudging your at-home work space to alleviate the accumulation of negative energies in the area.

The Living Room

The living room can tell you a lot about your life, both physically and spiritually. Examine your living room; is it cluttered, in disarray, or orderly? Is it a reflection of your values and purpose in life? Does it allow you to reflect your relationship with the Divine? If it seems something is amiss—too much chaos, not enough comfort, or too much crowding—it can suggest a physical and spiritual imbalance in your life. For example, a lack or absence of plants might suggest that you are lacking earth energies or you need to be more grounded. An overabundance of books piled everywhere might suggest that you have an overabundance of air qualities. Consider decorative and functional changes to this space to help promote greater balance in your mundane and spiritual existence.

The living room is a place where you spend a lot of time interacting with your loved ones, friends, and family members. Symbolically, this room is associated with your personality, your likes and dislikes, and the conscious mind. The living area is one of the main rooms in your home that your guests will see, so it is a room that represents you on a superficial level only, or how you present yourself to others. If you look around your living room and find an array of objects that belong in other rooms, this could be indicative that other areas of your daily life are becoming intrusive, affecting your freedom and space.

Closets

Closets are secreted inner spaces where you store clothing and supplies. These areas should not be neglected and they need to be readily cleansed. Closets symbolize secrets and physical organization. Based on the principle, "As within, so without," you become more spirituality centered and organized if you are physically centered and organized. Time spent clearing/smudging the home, including closet areas, should include the active cleaning, organizing, and setting aside unneeded or unused items for donation or contribution.

Consider the urge to hoard and avoid items that pile up in the space as akin to the accumulation of physical and spiritual residue. Just as energy residue can manifest in physical blocks and illnesses, so can accumulation of unused or forgotten stuff contribute to stagnation. It is no wonder the phrase "cleaning out my closet" is used as a metaphor for soul-searching. Being mindful in this practice can keep you free from undue residual stress and help alleviate energy stagnation. Similar care should be applied to basement areas, attics, and forgotten spaces in your home.

Bedroom

Love, passion, rest, slumber, and psychic dreams are all associated with the bedroom. Of all the places in your home, the room to which you retire for peace and rest should emanate with comforting energies. Sometimes the bedroom becomes an all-purpose room, where you end up reading, watching television, studying, and storing your valuables, too. In many cases, you may find that the objects and things that take over your bedroom space represent the intrusion of external demands, distractions, the encroaching upon your space, all of which end up upsetting the equilibrium of your private space.

Create a peaceful atmosphere in your bedroom conducive to rest and dream work. Soft, cool, soothing colors and lighting work best in this kind of room. You can enjoy calming scents such as lavender or jasmine to promote an atmosphere of tranquility. Place guardian totems or fae figurines within the room to buffer the area from negativity and negative energies from the mundane world. Accentuate the space with reminders of harmony and/or intimacy. Roses, lilacs, and other flowery accents, not only make the room more aesthetically pleasing, but they carry the energies of Venus, Aphrodite, and other Goddesses of love. You can even add statuary, figurines, or pictures of Gods/Goddesses associated with romance, dreams, and sleep. You can fill the room with lunar energies too; open the curtains wide on moonlit nights and let the lunar light pour in or consecrate the room with consecrated lunar/moon water.

Den, Office, Workshop, and Studio

Some people work from home or engage in a creative hobby requiring workspace. You will need to cleanse your workspace regularly; strong and excessive focus, frustrations, the accumulation of concentrated energies, as well as the high volume of electronic usage can all contribute to the creation of chaotic energies, so much so, that an occasional clearing of the mundane workspace is required.

Place quartz or other stones near your computers or electronics to absorb the excess energies created through their use. It may also be helpful if you lace reminders of the Goddess/God whose aspect most embodies the focus of your work in your workspace as well. For example, a musical rehearsal space or a healing space might have symbols of Apollo, or a writing studio might have symbols associated with Thoth, the Egyptian God of Writing or Athena, the Greek Goddess of Wisdom.

The inclusion of animal totems that embody the skills you need to see the successful completion of your work can also prove beneficial. For instance, writers might benefit from having feathers nearby as they work: they are not only symbolic of writing, but feathers are also reminders of Bird of Prey Goddesses like Isis and Nephthys in the Egyptian pantheon. Fox animal totems are ideal for anyone whose enterprise thrives on clever business dealings since the fox is shrewd, swift, and clever. As another example, if you are working in endeavors involving networking, a bee is an ideal animal totem since it symbolizes community, working together, and a hive mentality. Writing, as well as other creative blocks, can be addressed with the aid of spiritual tools. Incense, meditation, and trance work can be used to heighten creativity. If you need work solutions, the latter tools prove quite useful; even mandalas can be used to help you past creative blocks as well as to activate your natural intuition.

Patron Gods and Goddesses of the arts and music and totem animals can lend energies to boost your creative endeavors in the home work office or any room in the home. Consider keeping owl feathers nearby to inspire excellence in study and research or any kind of feathers for creative endeavors involving writing. Birds, frogs, and even dolphins are associated with sound and music, so they prove excellent as totems for such endeavors. Meanwhile, peacocks are associated with beauty, and swans are associated with grace, so they can serve as totem for endeavors calling for such attributes. Even if you are decorating a workout or exercise area, you can do so by using images of athletic, warrior-like deities such as Artemis, Athena, Isis, Morrigan, or Ares or animal totems like the tiger, bear, or wolf in order to represent the strength, endurance, and swiftness.

The Garden and Magickal Landscapes

Your life is Magickally enhanced with the earthy touch of nature provided by cultivating your own garden, whether the garden is in your yard or in several small pots on your windowsill. If space is limited, start small. Even limited physical space, with a little creativity, can be cultivated. Container gardens, hanging baskets, and small fountains can help to create a small, confined, sacred space indoors or out. In addition, potted herb gardens can deepen your connection to the earth while simultaneously allowing you to enjoy the contentment derived from successfully growing your own herbs. Consider enhancing the energies of potted herbs or plants by painting symbols on the plant/herb containers with the intention of helping the plants/herbs have greater healing powers or with the intention of helping the plants thrive. You can charge ordinary tap water with the specific intent to help your plants grow healthy and strong too. You can also place statues or figurines of animal totems of protection around your plants or gardening space.

In larger gardens, you can place décor and protective items that will help in drawing positive energies to your space. You can hang wind chimes charged for protection from a hook or you can hang a gong in the garden; this especially beneficial if you plan to meditate in the same area. You might want to create a gardening area that draws butterflies, hummingbirds, or even bees to promote the pollination of your garden. Around the outer boundary of your garden, you can place crystals, stones, coins, marbles, and the like since they prove attractive to the fae. You might want to give back to the natural environment for the gifts you receive from your garden; think about establishing bird feeders, squirrel feeders, and birdbaths nearby.

You can give honor to totem animals by placing figures, statues, or flags, signs and painted rocks displaying their likeness in your garden. Adding one or more gazing balls or witch balls to your garden décor allows you to integrate the perfect tool for scrying, contemplation, and meditation into your garden while simultaneously beautifying the area. You also have the option of creating a small altar area in the center of your garden and adding benches nearby for meditative practices.

You can leave offerings at the four corners of your garden area too, to thank the Divine for blessings or anything you harvest from the garden. Bear in mind that when you are leaving offerings for the Divine, they are partaking of the essence of the offering, and the physical offering will remain. You should therefore leave offerings that the natural wildlife can safely consume; when you leave offerings, be mindful of what physical creatures you might be unwittingly attracting to the area, and let common sense precautionary measures prevail.

When creating a large garden or sacred space outdoors, consider including an array of plants, herbs, flowers, and trees in your landscaping endeavors. Every plant/herb, flower, and tree has different Magickal correspondences and energies. Such energies and correspondences should be considered as you create your Magickal garden area. You should also align any figurines or statuary you choose with specific fertility or vegetation Gods and Goddesses to encourage the healthy growth of your garden/landscape area.

Negotiating Boundaries in Closed Quarters

Shared living space can bring out the need for tact and understanding, especially when you are looking to establish sacred space. When planning to move in with others, resist the decision to keep your religious practices a secret. This sets an unfair power dynamic into play right from the start and ensures an undercurrent of mistrust, secrecy, and dishonesty. The same honesty is called for when you are already living with others, and you desire to create a place of worship or a place where you can practice your Craft. In general, it is better to be up front about your practices and any special requests or needs you might have in terms of privacy before you move in with someone or before you begin practicing the Magickal arts in your home. It is more than appropriate to negotiate personal boundaries so that you can have the space/private time you require for practicing Magick and/or worship. If you are blessed with an area to designate as your sacred space, then make it clear to roommates, spouses, children, or visitors that the area needs to be respected. If necessary, explain that you want to preserve the positive energies of the area and that you want to keep your Magickal tools safe and/or out of the hands of children. If you are questioned about what your tools are or why you use them, be open, candid, and answer questions honestly.

Suppose your desire to practice Witchcraft begins after you are well-established in a home with others and everyone living with you has set routines, rooms, spaces, and beliefs. This kind of situation can be tricky. If you are just learning the Craft, take things gradually. You are just becoming comfortable with a new way of seeing the world, and sometimes it may take the people you reside with time to understand your viewpoint. In other instances, they may not understand your new practices at all and may actually frown upon your practices and/or beliefs.

You will have to discuss your needs and feelings openly with those you live with; if you are going to practice Witchcraft in your home, you cannot and should not avoid this kind of discussion. If you are living with others that are willing to communicate with you, to listen to your point of view, and to discuss the issue of establishing a private area and private time for your worship/Magickal practices, you are in luck. It is hoped that you will be able to negotiate a mutual understanding where everyone will respect each other's beliefs and allow room for everyone to partake of their own beliefs and practices. If, however, you are living with people who are not at all open to the idea of you practicing Witchcraft in the space that you share with them, then, as unfair as it may seem, you will have to turn to other alternatives. You do not want to practice your Craft in a place where an undercurrent of negativity can arise or exist. In the event that you are residing with others that may not like the idea of having you practice witchcraft in the home, you might want to consider practicing with other local practitioners or covens that are sometimes more than willing to share established sacred space. You can also consider partaking of Magickal practices outdoors. Finally, you have the option of establishing sacred space in the astral; to learn how to do so, see the end of this chapter.

Explaining the Magickal to the Mundane-Minded

The best explanation of who you are as a Witch is how you carry yourself as a person in your everyday life. People will not necessarily read the books you have read or attend the ceremonies you have attended. They will, however, observe you and draw conclusions based on what is presented to them through your words and actions. First, it is necessary to live by what you believe, and let your practices and spirituality show in how you behave as well as in what you say.

Beyond this, always consider to who and why you need further self-disclosure. Some of us are approached outright and questioned, interrogated, attacked, or accused of being something we are not because of our choice in clothing, jewelry, or reading material. You will have to consider the best response for a given situation. A person behaving in a hostile or aggressive manner is not likely to be transformed into a person who is less hostile or aggressive, no matter what you say or do. Sometimes it is not worth wasting the energy engaging in a battle over religious understandings or the lack thereof.

Other times, individuals in the workplace, in the family, in an apartment building, or in the neighborhood may take notice of your beliefs and practices. They, in turn, may have questions about what you do. The amount of your personal life that you share with others is, of course, at your own discretion, but you might find that you are more than ready to provide curious individuals with honest responses. Consider the essentials of Witchcraft, Wicca, and/or paganism. Can you summarize what these things mean? If not, you might want to practice summarizing your belief system so that it can be readily digested by your audience. If you tell anyone about your beliefs and practices, you will want to do so confidently without fostering confusion. The people you speak with should not feel overwhelmed by the information you share, but should be able to walk away with a solid understanding of what you have explained to them.

For the rational and reasonable, it will only be a matter of time before it is obvious that your Magickal practices are the least of any community's concern. For the irrational or unreasonable, you are not going to change their mindset. If harassment occurs at work or home, no matter how tempting it is to lash out, keep your senses clear, remain calm, and document the event. Make sure you record the date, time, and exactly what occurred. Whether you have employed Magickal protections or not, sometimes you have to make the decision to contact those in authority to report the incident. Consult local legal aid if necessary and enlist the help of other like-minded people in the neighborhood or community as well.

How you explain your Magickal practices to non-practitioners will depend on how the person reacts to you. If the individual is illustrating an interest in your beliefs and practices, try to answer questions as openly and honestly as you can. As you speak make sure you convey your practices to the individual; you should use the appropriate terminology associated with your practices and thoroughly explain what those terms mean. For example, if you talk about skyclad practices or sabbats, take the extra time to explain what those words mean in relation to Magickal practices. In addition, always bear in mind as you share your beliefs with another, the goal of your conversation is not conversion, but open communication that leads to the development of understanding.

If you want to be respected for your beliefs and practices, you cannot be rude or disrespectful when you are speaking to another about your practices. To be respected, you must give respect in return.

Alternatively, if a person is not really genuinely interested in developing an understanding of who you are and your belief system, and the individual is only trying to goad you into an argument or confrontation, again this is not a call for disrespect on your part. Instead, keep in the back of your mind that you do not have to justify your belief system to anyone and you have the right to live your life as you choose to live it. One of the most powerful tools you'll develop as a witch is the ability to not let your emotions rule what it is you say or what you do, especially when it is in response to another person's words and/or actions.

Temporary Housing and Dorms

If you find yourself temporarily living in a group home, shelter or in another temporary setting, it may be more challenging to carry out your practices. Crisis can occur to any of us at any time and when you need your connection to the God/Goddess the most, you may also need to be the most creative in how your needs are met. Sometimes, your Magickal tools will not even be allowed in certain settings and it is highly unlikely that you will be able to establish an altar or sacred space of your own. First, follow the rules of the residence if in fact you want to live there. It is unfair, unwise, and unethical to break the rules of the establishment just because you do not like them.

In a pinch, you do not need physical tools because Magick comes from within, and wherever you are, you are with the Divine. You do not need anyone's permission to communicate with the God/Goddess. Even if you are in a temporary setting, you have the ability to remain deeply connected to the Divine at all times. This part of your Magickal/spiritual quest challenges you to connect to the spirit with minimal trappings; accept the challenge and know it is a temporary test.

Alternatively, residency in a dorm is a choice; a college education is a luxury, a privilege, and partaking of campus-based housing subjects you to the regulations established by the educational institution. You may have little choice in selecting a dorm or roommates. Become educated in campus polices regarding religious practices, the use of candles, sharp tools, and the like. You may need to modify your altar or Magickal accessories while you live in a dorm setting. In fact, this is the type of setting that is probably better for the use of portable or hide-away altars. You also have to consider how much you really want to expose your sacred objects to a dorm lifestyle; consider that not everyone will be as respectful of your beliefs and tools as you are. Sometimes dorm life can also be filled with social pressures and drama, generating an energy you definitely do not want associated with your sacred tools.

You may have to limit the tools you use while in the dorm, and you will have to be respectful of other people's beliefs. In truth, practicing Magick in a dorm setting is often not conducive to Magickal practices. Instead, you might want to make a practice of creating sacred space outdoors, in a private area, or conducting your Magickal practices when you are not on campus. Again, you also have the option of establishing sacred space in an astral temple as an alternative.

Circle Casting

Whether you practice Magick indoors or out, before any ritual workings, you have to prepare the area so that you can cast a Magick circle. The area where you plan to work is influenced by the day-to-day energies it is exposed to; sometimes negative energy can accumulate or taint the existing energies of an area, even if the site you have chosen has been used for ritual purposes before.

The area you choose for your sacred space needs to be cleaned both physically and spiritually. If you are arranging an area for your altar for the first time, you will want to make sure the entire area has been thoroughly cleaned from top to bottom before you erect your altar and begin placing your sacred tools on it. If your altar is already established, you need to implement a regular cleaning routine of your sacred space.

After you have physically gone through the area, then you will need to turn your attention to the spiritual cleansing of the area in order to make sure it is fit for use in rituals and Magickal applications. There are many ways you can spiritually cleanse your space. A practitioner might use a besom to clear out all negative energies through a physical sweeping action. While sweeping the besom back and forth from East to West, you can visualize negativity being forcefully swept out of the area. Some practitioners prefer to perform the Lesser Banishing Ritual of the Pentagram for clearing an area for the creation of sacred space.

Allowing Entry in the Magick Circle

Some covens like using an entry rite before allowing practitioners to enter the area where a circle casting will be performed. The entry rite requires that a practitioner request permission to enter sacred space, and permission is granted from an individual chosen to be in charge of allowing entry into the sacred area. You can use an entry rite of your choosing, you can write your own entry rite, or you can use the one presented here if you desire.

Entry Rite

Priest/Priestess/Practitioner: *Who stands here at the threshold of this world and the realm of Magick, seeking entrance to this sacred site, and what is your purpose here?*

Practitioner: *I (name/witch name), come here seeking to give reverence to the God and Goddess, and to bear witness to great mysteries.*

Priest/Priestess/Practitioner: *Then as the gatekeeper who stands guard between the worlds I bid you, my witch brother/sister entrance. You are welcome here for you are one of our own.*

Circle Casting Ritual

Light an incense of your choice before you cast circle. Light all of the candles on your altar as you move in a deosil (clockwise) direction from East to North. Once the candles are lit, return to the front of your altar. Face the East. Take up the incense and hold it high. Say:

I am the air, the mover of thoughts and will,
I am the beginning and I am renewal,
I refresh the soul and carry it beyond death,
By me great mysteries are known.

Replace the incense on the altar (as you move through the ritual, return each object before you take up the next). Turn to the South. Take up the athame and hold it high. Say:

I am the fire, spark of inspiration and life,
My flames burn away impurities; all I touch is transformed.
My warmth nurtures the soul; I illuminate truth,
By me all Magick is wrought.

Turn to the West. Hold up the chalice high. Say:

I am Water, the life-blood of Mother Earth,
With the power to cleanse, purify, nourish, and refresh,
I am the mirror of the past, present, future, the mind, and what lies beyond,
By me divine secrets are revealed.

Turn to the North. Hold the bowl of salt high. Say:

I am the Earth, strong, solid, steadfast, and true,
I stand sentinel witnessing and remembering all,
I heal by plant and herb; my memory is of soil and stone,
By me the living are nourished and the dead embraced.

Turn and face the midpoint between North and East. Take up the pentacle and hold it high. Say:

I am Akasha, the final point of the pentacle,
Bringing together the elements,
To birth a fifth, stronger together than alone,
By me Earth, Fire, Water, and Air are one.

Replace the pentacle on the altar, and take up your censer. From your position in front of the altar move deosil to the East. Draw a pentacle in air with the incense; visualize it expanding, growing larger, and rushing out into infinite space. Say:

In the East with scented smoke,
The power of air I invoke.

From your position, move to the South. Repeat the visualization you did in the East. Say:

In the South with scented smoke,
The power of fire I invoke.

From your position, move to the West. Repeat the visualization. Say:

In the West with scented smoke,
The power of water I invoke.

From your position, move to the North. Repeat the visualization. Say:

In the North with scented smoke,
The power of earth I invoke.

Move in a deosil direction, return to the front of your altar. Take up your athame, and continue in a deosil direction to the East. Repeat the following chant as you move slowly from to the East, to South, to West to North, and return to your starting point in the East. Hold the athame in your left hand and hold your arm straight out as you walk the circle. (If you are constructing the circle with other practitioners, make sure there is ample room for you to move around the circle with the athame without injuring anyone.) Say:

Mother, Maiden, and Crone,
Hear the words I intone,
Father, Sage, and Son,
This circle casting has begun.
Ancestors, Guardians, and Elements four,
Your presence here I implore.
Protect me now in this place,
Now transformed to sacred space.

Remain in the East; take up the bell and your staff. Ring the bell three times, and say:

Guardians of the East join us now,
Protect this circle inside and out.

Use your staff to tap on the floor three times. Repeat this process at each corner, making sure you change the identification of the corner when you speak.

Return to the front of the altar and set down the bell and staff. Outstretch your arms and address the Universe. Say:

Guardians Above, Below, Of far and near,
Guard and protect this Magickal sphere.
The circle has been cast.

Circle Closing

When you are done with your ritual or Magickal workings, you will need to close the circle. Begin at the front of your altar; move deosil to the East. You will repeat the following process at each cardinal point.

Tap your staff on the floor three times. Say:

Guardians of the East, I honor thee.
Thank you for attending our Magickal rite,
Go or remain in peace, love, and light.

Ring the bell three times. Allow the final ring to fade away completely before moving to the next point in the circle. After doing the final recitation in the North corner, return to the front of the altar. Again, tap your staff on the floor three times. Address the Universe and say:

Guardians Above, Below, of far and near,
We thank you for your presence here.
Go in peace, love, and light,
As we call the end to this rite.

Ring the bell three times, and allow the sound to fade. Say:

The circle is released,
So mote it be, blessed be.

Circle Closing Versus Leaving the Circle Constructed

When you cast circle to perform a ritual, you take the circle down when you are done with the working. Sometimes, however, it is necessary for you to leave the circle up. For example, if you feel that you are not well protected or if you feel there are negative energies lingering, you can request that the guardians remain as long as they feel it necessary to do so. Make sure you are respectful when making such a request, and understand that it is of the free will of the Guardians to remain or leave. If you are seeking additional methods for protecting your home, there are several rituals and spells provided here for adaptation and use.

Additional Spells / Rituals for Protecting Your Sacred Space

Spells are easy to perform, and they are one of the easiest ways to help protect your home and/or sacred areas. You can conduct spells to improve the energies in your home, to keep your home protected from malevolent energies, or to cleanse each room spiritually. Here we share some simple spells for use in the home that you can use or adapt as you see fit.

Home Invisibility I

This is an excellent spell for when you do not want visitors or if you do not want your home easily visible to negative energies. You can chant this spell while empowering wind chimes or other home ornamentations. You can then hang the chimes or decoration up in your home to serve as a permanent fixture for warding off negative.

I call upon the primal powers,
On this day, at this hour,
Mist and shadow, darkness and cloud,
Wrap my home in darkened shroud.
Hide me and mine from those that mean me harm,
My home and family made safe by this charm.

Home Invisibility II

Take a moment to visualize your home blending in with Mother Nature until it fades into the background. While speaking this spell, you need to walk the perimeter of your property. As you walk, say:

Powers of the elements rise,
Now unseen across the skies,
Surround my home that it may be,
Safe from prying eyes who see.
Let it blend into nature's own,
Let it be safe, my sacred home,
No bane may find it, this is clear,
I no longer have to fear.
For we are hidden from those who seek,
From ocean's depth to mountain's peak,
From desert's sands and city's land,
The powers cover us with protective hands.
From high above and far below,
My home is safe, of this I know,
Thank you for your shielding light,
Thank you for your will and might,
For this is all I ask of thee,
As I will, so mote it be!

Basic Protection Spell

Horus and Isis, to my home fortification bring,
Isis and Nephthys, spread your protective wings,
Great God Ra, on my dwelling you do shine,
Osiris, allow only the entrance of spirits benign.
Lady Hathor, keep my critters safe and sound,
and bring to my home joy abound,
Goddess Sekhmet, She who, in evil, instills fear,
Keep my home free of bane, of pain, and sorrowful tear.

Home Protection Spell

Visualize all within and around your home in a protective bubble of white light. Visualize spirit guardians posed at the four corners of entryways, and say:

From forces astral and mundane,
This house is protected and so remains,
Always stable, safe, and secure,
Negative will not cross these doors.

Home Cleansing I

Light a smudge stick or some sage. Walk around the circumference of your home, moving in a clockwise, or deosil, direction, as you carry the smudge stick or incense with you. Say:

From Eastern Corner, to South, to West, to North,
All evil energies I herein cast forth,
Out of my home and into the abyss,
My home be filled with joy and bliss.
This entire dwelling now be blessed,
This house liberated from trial and test.
Negativity is welcome here no more,
From corner to corner and rooftop to floor.
The love of the Lady and Lord instilled in this space,
Banishing negative, leaving positive in its place.
No evil shall remain,
No malevolence retained,

My home abundant with sacred light,
Dissonant energies at once reunite.
As I will it, so shall it be.

Home Cleansing II

For this cleansing, you will need your cauldron, a wooden spoon, the protective herbs of your choosing, and consecrated water. If you do not have a cauldron, you can use a gypsy pot or a large glass bowl. You will also need a small amount of vinegar in a bowl. Make sure all of your tools have been consecrated before you begin.

Sit in a quiet place with all of your tools laid out in front of you; sitting on the floor is perfectly fine. Relax and take in a few deep breaths. Next, pour the consecrated water into your cauldron or bowl and say:

I pour this water to cleanse and free,
This house of bane and negativity.

Add herbs to the vinegar. Say:

Mother Earth I call to thee,
To clear this house and set us free,
Remove all negative that you see,
Bind this house in positivity.

Pour the vinegar and herbs into the cauldron. Mix the ingredients with the wooden spoon while stirring in a deosil (clockwise) direction. Repeat the following three time as you stir:

Stirring, stirring, round and round,
No more negative to be found.

When finished, you will need to spread the mixture around your home. If you have a large cauldron, you can transfer the mixture into a cup or bowl. Start at the front door and move clockwise through your house. Use the index finger on your projective hand to dip into the mixture and draw a pentacle in front of every door, window, and mirror in your home, dipping your finger in the mixture for each entry you Magickally seal. Take the remainder of the mixture outdoors and evenly disperse it at the four corners of the house or property.

Protection from Malevolent Energies Spell

This is a simple spell you can use to banish negative energies in your home. Use your favorite incense and burn a white and black candle. Say:

Triple Goddess I call to thee,
Help me now by power of three,
To clear my hearth and home this night,
Making negative spirits take flight,
To send them back from whence they came,
And let them burn in red hot flames,
Never to return onto me,
By my will, so mote it be.

Protection from Malevolent Energies Ritual

For this ritual, you will need a black, white, gold, and silver candle. You will also need your athame, wand, a smudge stick or an incense burner, and some sage. In addition, you will need four very small cups and some white vinegar. You can perform this ritual in front of your altar, but it can be performed anywhere.

Charge the black candle to absorb all negative energies, and the white candle for filling the room with positive energies. The gold and silver candles represent the dual power of the Divine. Set up all four candles on a sturdy surface and light them. Lay out your other tools so they are ready for use when you need them.

Take up the athame and make a pentacle in the air. As you draw the pentacle, visualize it blazing with fire. Visualize the pentacle expanding to encompass the entire room, home, or area. See the outermost points of the pentacle extending to the ends of the universe. Say:

The pentacle is drawn by the athame,
I banish evil spirits both nameless and named.

If you know of specific sources of negativity that may be aimed in your direction, name them aloud now.

Now take up the wand. Draw a pentacle in the air, again seeing a flame forming from the end of your wand as you draw the pentacle in front of you. Visualize the expansion of the pentacle; once again, see the outermost points of the pentacle extending to the ends of the universe. Say:

The pentacle is drawn by wand empowered,
All malicious energies herein devoured.

Draw a pentacle with your forefinger in the air in front of you; see the pentacle forming out of flames coming from your forefinger as you draw it. Say:

The pentacle is drawn by my own hand,
All evil be gone at my command.

Set out a small glass full of white vinegar in the farthest four corners of the area you are looking to protect; vinegar is acidic and acts as a natural drying agent, thereby making it less feasible for spirits to manifest. You do not require a large amount: a shot glass with a spoonful or two of vinegar will suffice. After setting out vinegar in the four corners, begin at the front door of your home. Move in a clockwise direction and go from room to room while burning some fresh sage or a smudge stick. As you walk, repeat these words until you have circled every room in your home three times:

By smoldering fire and scented smoke,
Divine powers of protection are herein invoked!
This space be filled with happiness and bliss,
All that is negative is herein dismissed.

Now take the burning smudge stick and go to every door, window, and mirror in the home, making the sign of the pentacle at every opening in the home with the smudge stick and smoke. As you make each pentacle say:

These earthly entry ways no passage provide,
To spiritual energies serving to divide.

Astral Temple

The physical sanctuary is limited to physical space and material belongings. When there is no ideal place to establish sacred space in the physical, it can still be created in the astral: another plane of existence to where the soul/spirit can travel at will via meditation and/or out of body experience. The astral temple is only limited by your ability to focus and visualize, and your creativity.

You can write your own astral temple meditation or you can use guided meditations to learn how to create the temple. The different designs of temple construction are limitless; you can elaborate on the design any way you see fit to do so. You can also create a meditation "trigger" so that you can return to this meditation repeatedly. You can try the following astral temple meditation whenever you want to create sacred space in the astral.

Astral Temple Meditation

Sit in a chair and relax. Make sure you are completely comfortable. Close your eyes and ease into a relaxed state by focusing on the breath. With each breath, you are becoming open to the psychic, astral energies around you. Continue to concentrate on your breathing as you become more and more relaxed.

When you are completely relaxed, in your mind's eye, see the surrounding room begin to blur. Watch the physicality of the room slowly fade as it is replaced by a cool, thick, relaxing mist. Watch as the mist turns into thick, swirling fog surrounding you on all sides. Relax and enjoy this tranquil place, free of mundane distractions and commotion.

Now watch as the fog begins to drift away. As the fog slowly clears, you find that you are surrounded by a stunning outdoor scene: one that is calming and vibrant. It is here that you meet your astral guide or spirit guide, who will walk with you as you travel to your sacred temple, answer your questions, and who will offer you seeds of wisdom to carry with you on your journey. Make a note of anything your guide shares with you for later reflection.

You can feel the sacred energies coursing all around you, mingling with your own energies, and then coursing back into the external environment. You feel intimately connected to this place, like you have always known it, and you feel the sense of coming home. You can intuitively sense the presence of the Goddess and God here, as you take in all the natural colors, shapes, smells, and the exquisite landscape. You feel a sense of peace you have never known before, and you know that upon your return to the physical, this inner peace will be carried with you as you go forth into the mundane world.

Take another look around and you see a path before you. When you are ready to proceed, you head toward the path that leads to stairs ascending into the clouds, beyond your sight. You begin to climb the stairs, effortlessly moving from one step to the next, until you reach the clouds. Moving through the clouds, you reach a place where the clouds part, and reveal a sacred temple in the distance. You walk toward the structure aware that the temple holds valuable mysteries, and powerful energies. You also know that this place is made only for you, your sacred self, and that no undesirable energies or entities can enter without your consent. Here, you can work your Magickal workings without interference, disturbance, or disruption: you are safe inside the walls of your sacred temple.

As you draw nearer to the temple, your astral guide stops and advises you that he or she can go no further; the temple is your space alone. Before you can enter the temple, you see a stream of clear flowing water encircling the entire structure. You must enter this water to wash away any remaining residual energies and to purify yourself before you can enter your temple structure. You enter the cool water: it is refreshing, and you are completely comfortable as any negative emotions, thoughts, or energies are cleansed away.

Following your purification, you walk up to the entrance of the temple fully knowing that the inner workings of the structure change based on spiritual need, and that every time you return to the temple the interior of the structure is different. You place your hand on the door and the door automatically opens for you.

You enter the temple and the door quickly closes behind you. Inside your temple, you house a massive library of Magickal information, rituals, spells, memories, and files, all of which you control the access to so you can tap into their knowledge whenever you need to do so. It is here you have the ability to use the astral versions of any physical tools you may own, and you may find that your inner temple looks a lot like your physical altar set up in the mundane realm. Here you can perform Magickal workings simply through visualization and you know your Magick is just as powerful in the astral as in the physical.

In the astral, you can allow yourself to freely shapeshift as well, allowing different parts of your spirit to surface in animal form. Make a note of any animal forms your spirit takes; this form may provide you with messages that can enhance your day-to-day existence or it can serve as an animal totem. You intuitively know that you can access this temple any time you are in need of sacred space.

When you are done with your Magickal workings, you can walk across the temple to another door. When you place your hand on the door, it opens up to an area filled with the thick, misty fog you first encountered as the realm of the mundane and the astral united. As the fog slowly clears, the physicality of the room you are in begins to reemerge slowly. You feel light, refreshed, awake, and alert. You are able to remember everything you encountered with clarity.

Conclusion

With a little practice, awareness, and creativity, just about any mundane tool can have a Magickal use and almost any space can be transformed into sacred space. What's more, your sacred space does not have to be confined to one small area in your home. Once mundane tools are made Magickal or sacred space is established, the tools and space should always be treated with the utmost respect. In honoring your space and tools, you are honoring extensions of yourself while simultaneously safeguarding the Magickal energies that your tools and space accumulate. Finally, while witchly trappings are wonderful to have, one final fact is of the highest importance: Magick comes from within you; your mind is the most powerful Magickal tool you will ever possess, and no physical tools or space are ever needed in order to have successful Magickal workings.

Endnotes

Introduction

[1-3]John Harland and T. T. Wilkinson, eds. *Lancashire Folk-Lore: Illustrative of the Superstitious Beliefs and Practices, Local Customs, and Usages of the People of the County* Palatine (London: Frederic Warne and Co., 1867), 151.

[4]Walter William Skeat, *The Science of Etymology* (Oxford: Clarendon Press, 1912), 1-14.

[5]Walter William Skeat, "Anoint," in *A Concise Etymological Dictionary of the English Language*, new ed., by Walter William Skeat (Oxford: Clarendon Press, 1901), 19.

Chapter 1

[1]*Oxford English Dictionary Online, 1989 ed.*, s.v. "altar," accessed June 18, 2011, last modified June 2011, http://www.oed.com/view/Entry/5752.

[2]Austen Henry Layard, *Nineveh and Babylon: A Narrative of a Second Expedition* (London: John Murray, 1867), 40-66.

[3]James Bonwick, Egyptian Belief and Modern Thought (London: C. Kegan Paul and Co., 1878), 206-224.

[4]John Romilly Allen, *The Reliquary and Illustrated Archæologist* (London: Bemrose and Sons, Limited, 1900), 226-241.

[5]Exod. 39:23-26 (RSV).

[6-7]Thomas Worth, *English Bells and Bell Lore: A Book on Bells*, ed. William Beresford (Leek: T. Mark, 1888), 192-203.

[8]*Oxford English Dictionary Online*, 1989 ed., s.v. "bell," accessed June 18, 2011, last modified June 2011, http://www.oed.com/view/Entry/17406.

[9]James Donald, ed., *Chamber's Etymological Dictionary of the English Language* (London and Edinburgh: W and R. Chambers, 1867), s.v. "Bowline."

[10]Hensleigh Wedgewood, "Bor-Burin," in *A Dictionary of English Etymology*, vol. 1 of A-D (London: Trübner and Co., 1859), 202.

[11]Harry Wilson, *Why and Wherefore? Simple Explanations of the Ornaments, Vestments, and Ritual of the Church* (Milwaukee, Wisconsin: The Young Churchman Co., 1897), 49-50.

[12]*Oxford English Dictionary Online*, 1989 ed., s.v. "capnomancy," accessed June 18, 2011, last modified June 2011, http://www.oed.com/view/Entry/27500.

[13]Colin Macfarquhar and George Gleig, eds., *Encyclopædia Britannica or A Dictionary of Arts, Sciences, and Miscellaneous Literature*, 3rd ed. (Edinburgh: University of Michigan, 1797), I V, s.v. "Capnomancy."

[14]Charles Mackay LL.D, *Memoirs of Extraordinary Popular Delusions* (New York: Office of the National Illustrated Library, 1852), 1:252.

[15]Benjamin Eli Smith A.M., L.H.D, "Libanomancy," in *The Century Dictionary and Cyclopedia: An Encyclopedic Lexicon of the English Language*, rev. ed., ed. William Dwight Whitney Ph.D., LL.D (New York: The Century Co, 1911), 5:3431.

[16]Charles Mackay LL.D, *Memoirs of Extraordinary Popular Delusions* (New York: Office of the National Illustrated Library, 1852), 1:265.

[17]Charles Storrs Halsey, *An Etymology of Latin and Greek* (Boston: Ginn, Heath, and Co., 1882), 179.

[18-20]Henry Clay Trumbull, *The Covenant of Salt: As Based on The Significance and Symbolism of Salt in Primitive Thought* (New York: Charles Scribner's Sons, 1899), 53-107.

[21]Gen. 19:26 (RSV).

[22]*Oxford English Dictionary Online, 1989 ed.*, s.v. "wand," accessed June 18, 2011, last modified June 2011, http://www.oed.com/view/Entry/225430.

[23]Charles G Herbermann Ph.D., LL.D., et al., eds., *The Catholic Encyclopedia: an International Work of Reference on the Constitution, Doctrine, Discipline, and History of the Catholic Church* (New York: Robert Appleton Company, 1909), 5, s.v. "Egypt - Ancient Egyptian Religion."

[24]Dudley Wright, "The Affinity of Druidism with Other Religions," *The Open Court*, January 1921, 129-141.

[25]Walter Lowrie, *Monuments of the Early Church* (New York: The MacMillan Company, 1906), 213-214.

[26]Maurice A Canney, "Wand, Magic," in *An Encyclopædia of Religions* (London: George Routledge and Sons, Ltd., 1921), 382.

[27]Anne Jirsch, *Cosmic Energy: How to Harness the Invisible Power Around You to Transform Your Life* (Woodbury, Minnesota: Llewellyn Publications, 2010), 1-9.

Chapter 2

Walter William Skeat, "Rune," in *A Concise Etymological Dictionary of the English Language* (New York: Harper and Brothers, 1882), 409.

[2]William Dwight Whitney, "Amulet," in *The Century Dictionary and Cyclopedia* (New York: The Century Co., 1906), Volume I: 189.

[3]George Fredrick Kunz, *The Curious Lore of Precious Stones* (Philadelphia: J. B. Uppincott Company, 1913), 19-50.

[4]Abram Smythe Palmer, "Talisman," in *Folk-Etymology: A Dictionary of Verbal Corruptions or Words Perverted in Form or Meaning by False Derivation or Mistaken Analogy* (London: George Bell and Sons, 1882), 606.

[5]Charles John Smith, "Talisman," in *Synonyms Discriminated: A Dictionary of Synonymous Words in the English Language*, ed. Henry Percy Smith (New York: Henry Hold and Company, 1904), 713.

[6]George Edwin Rines, ed., *The Encyclopedia Americana: A Library of Universal Knowledge* (New York: The

Encyclopedia Americana Corporation, 1918), Vol 1, s.v. "Amulet."

[7]Leopold Claremont, *The Gem-Cutter's Craft* (London: George Bell and Sons, 1906), 82-90.

[8]John Ogilivie, "Besom," in *The Imperial Dictionary of the English Language: A Complete Encyclopedic Lexicon, Literary, Scientific, and Technological*, new ed., ed. Charles Annadale (London: Blackie and Sons, 1882), 261.

[9]James A.H. Murray, ed., *A New English Dictionary on Historical Principles*, part iii ed. (Oxford: Macmillan and Co., 1887), Part III Batter-Boz, s.v. "Besom."

[10]John Ogilivie, "Besom," in *The Imperial Dictionary of the English Language: A Complete Encyclopedic Lexicon,* Literary, Scientific, and Technological, new ed., ed. Charles Annadale (London: Blackie and Sons, 1882), 261.

[11]Ebenezer Cobham Brewer, "Snuffer," in *Etymological and Pronouncing Dictionary of Difficult Words* (London: Ward, Lock, and Co., Warwick House, 1882), 1150.

[12]Hensleigh Wedgwood, "Cauldron," in *A Dictionary of English Etymology*, vol. 3 of A-D (London: Trübner and Co., 1859), 313.

[13]Hensleigh Wedgwood, "Cord," in *A Dictionary of English Etymology*, vol. 3 of A-D (London: Trübner and Co., 1859), 377.

[14]Hensleigh Wedgwood, "Mortar," in *Dictionary of English Etymology*, vol. 2 of E-P (London: Trübner and Co, 1862), 424.

[15]W. M. Ahern, "A Pharmaco-Philological Medley," *Pharmaceutical Record and Weekly Review* VI (January-February 1886): 155.

[16]Walter William Skeat, "Pupa," in *A Concise Etymological Dictionary of the English Language* (New York: Harper and Brothers, 1882), 379.

[17]Abram Smythe Palmer, "Poppet," in *Folk-Etymology: A Dictionary of Verbal Corruptions or Words Perverted in Form or Meaning By False Derivation or Mistaken Analogy* (London: George Bell and Sons, 1882), 215.

[18]John Gardner Wilkinson, *A Popular Account of the Egyptians*, rev ed. (New York: Harper and Brothers, 1854), 264-266.

[19]Arthur Hamilton Smith, *A Guide to the Department of Greek and Roman Antiquities in the British Museum* (London: British Museum Department of Greek and Roman Antiquities, 1899), 145.

[20]*The Encylopædia Britannica: A Dictionary of Arts, Sciences, Literature, and General Information*, 11th ed., s.v. "Ceramics," by Robert Lockhart Hobson.

[21]Walter William Skeat, "Potion," in *A Concise Etymological Dictionary of the English Language* (Oxford: Macmillan and Co., 1882), 367.

[22]John Craig, "Sigil," in A *New Universal Etymological and Pronouncing Dictionary of Embracing All The Terms, Used in Art, Science, and Literature: Embracing All the Terms Used in Art, Science, and Literature* (London: Henry George Collins, 1849), 2:687.

[23]Walter William Skeat, "Statue," in *A Concise Etymological Dictionary of the English Language* (Oxford: Macmillan and Co., 1882), 467.

[24]*Report and Transactions of the Devonshire Association for the Advancement of Science and Art*, 2nd ser (Plymouth: W. Brendon and Son, 1900), 89-90.

[25]Cora Linn Daniels and Charles McClellan Stevens, eds. Encyclopædia of Superstitions, Folklore, and the Occult *Sciences of the World: A Comprehensive Library of Human Belief and Practice in the Mysteries of Life* (Chicago: J. H. Yewdale and Sons, 1903), 3:1446-1450.

[26]Cora Linn Daniels and Charles McClellan Stevens, eds. *Encyclopedia of Superstitions, Folklore, and the Occult Sciences of the World: A Comprehensive Library of Human Belief and Practice in the Mysteries of Life* (Chicago: J. H. Yewdale and Sons, 1903), 3:1446-1450.

Chapter 3

[1]Walter William Skeat, "Chimes," in *A Concise Etymological Dictionary of the English Language* (Oxford: Macmillan and Co., 1882), 107.

[2]William Dwight Whitney, ed., *The Century Dictionary: An Encyclopedic Lexicon of the English Language*, vol. 3 of Volume III (New York: Century Co., 1906), s.v. "Gong."

[3]George Ripley and Charles A. Dana, eds., The *American Cyclopædia Volume X: Kinglet – Magnet*, 10th rev ed. (New York: D. Appleton and Company, 1875), s.v. "Labyrinth."

[4]James George Roche Forlong, *Faiths of Man: A Cyclopædia or Religions*, vol. 3 of *Vol III - N-Z* (London: Bernard Quaritch, 1906), s.v. "Rosary."

[5]Asiatic Society, ed. *Proceedings of the Asiatic Society of Bengal* (Calcutta: Asiatic Society, 1891), 189-191.

[6-7]James George Roche Forlong, *Faiths of Man: A Cyclopædia or Religions*, vol. 3 of *Vol III - N-Z* (London: Bernard Quaritch, 1906), s.v. "Rosary."

[8]Asiatic Society, ed. *Proceedings of the Asiatic Society of Bengal* (Calcutta: Asiatic Society, 1891), 189-191.

[9]Ernest John Eitel, "Mandala," in *Handbook of Chinese Buddhism: Being a Sanskrit-Chinese Dictionary with Vocabularies of Buddhist Terms*, 2nd rev. ed. (Hong Kong: Lane, Crawford and Co., 1888).

[10]Joseph Ernest De Becker, *Feudal Kamakura: Outline Sketch of the History of Kamakura* (Yokohama: Kelly and Walsh Ltd., 1907), 115-123.

[11]Ebenezer Coham Brewer, "Divination," in *Ward and Lock's Etymological and Pronouncing Dictionary of Difficult Words* (London: Ward, Lock and Co., 1852), 248.

[12]Walter William Skeat, "Pendulum," in *A Concise Etymological Dictionary of the English Language* (Oxford: Macmillan and Co., 1882), 341.

[13-14]Walter William Skeat, "Runes," in *A Concise Etymological Dictionary of the English Language* (Oxford: Macmillan and Co., 1882), 409.

[15]R. Chambers, *The Book of Days: A Miscellany of Popular Antiquities* (Edinburg: W. and R. Chambers, 1863), vol 1:281-284.

[16-17]Robert Hunter, "Astrology," in *Encyclopedic Dictionary: A New and Original Work of Reference to All the Words in the English Language*, vol. 1 of A-Cab (London: Cassell, Petter, Galpin, and Co., 1879), 333.

[18]Robert Hunter, "Astrology," in *Encyclopedic Dictionary: A New and Original Work of Reference to All the Words in the English Language*, vol. 1 of A-Cab (London: Cassell, Petter, Galpin, and Co., 1879), 333.

[19]Daniel Lyons PhD., "Stichomancy," in *The American Dictionary of the English Language*, ed. Daniel Lyons PhD. (New York: Peter Fenelon Collier, 1899), 414.

[20]James Stormonth, "Bibliomancy," in *Etymological Pronouncing Dictionary of The English Language*, 5th, rev. ed. (Edinburgh and London: William Blackwood and Sons, 1879), 47.

[21]John Craig, "Palmistry," in *A New Universal Technological, Etymological, and Pronouncing Dictionary of the English Language* (London: George Routledge and Co., 1852), 2:295-296.

Bibliography

Ahern, W. M. "A Pharmaco-Philological Medley." *Pharmaceutical Record and Weekly Review* VI (January-February 1886): 155.

Allen, John Romilly. *The Reliquary and Illustrated Archæologist*. London: Bemrose and Sons, Limited, 1900.

Asiatic Society, ed. *Proceedings of the Asiatic Society of Bengal*. Calcutta: Asiatic Society, 1891.

Bonwick, James. *Egyptian Belief and Modern Thought*. London: C. Kegan Paul and Co., 1878.

Brewer, Ebenezer Cobham. "Snuffer." In *Etymological and Pronouncing Dictionary of Difficult Words*. London: Ward, Lock, and Co., Warwick House, 1882.

Brewer, Ebenezer Coham. "Divination." In *Ward and Lock's Etymological and Pronouncing Dictionary of Difficult Words*. London: Ward, Lock and Co., 1852.

Canney, Maurice A. "Wand, Magic." In *An Encyclopaedia of Religions*. London: George Routledge and Sons, Ltd., 1921.

Chambers, R. *The Book of Days: A Miscellany of Popular Antiquities*. 1 Vols. Edinburg: W. and R. Chambers, 1863.

Claremont, Leopold. *The Gem-Cutter's Craft*. London: George Bell and Sons, 1906.

Craig, John. "Palmistry." In *A New Universal Technological, Etymological, and Pronouncing Dictionary of the English Language*. Vol. 2. London: George Routledge and Co., 1852.

———. "Sigil." In *A New Universal Etymological and Pronouncing Dictionary of Embracing All The Terms, Used in Art, Science, and Literature: Embracing All the Terms Used in Art, Science, and Literature*. Vol. 2. London: Henry George Collins, 1849.

Daniels, Cora Linn, and Charles McClellan Stevens, eds. *Encyclopedia of Superstitions, Folklore, and the Occult Sciences of the World: A Comprehensive Library of Human Belief and Practice in the Mysteries of Life*. Vol. 3. Chicago: J. H. Yewdale and Sons, 1903.

De Becker, Joseph Ernest. *Feudal Kamakura: Outline Sketch of the History of Kamakura*. Yokohama: Kelly and Walsh Ltd., 1907.

Donald, James, ed. *Chamber's Etymological Dictionary of the English Language*. London and Edinburgh: W and R. Chambers, 1867.

Eitel, Ernest John. "Mandala." In *Handbook of Chinese Buddhism: Being a Sanskrit-Chinese Dictionary with Vocabularies of Buddhist Terms*, 2nd rev. ed. Hong Kong: Lane, Crawford and Co., 1888.

Halsey, Charles Storrs. *An Etymology of Latin and Greek*. Boston: Ginn, Heath, and Co., 1882.

———. *An Etymology of Latin and Greek*. Boston: Ginn, Heath, and Co., 1882.

Harland, John, and T. T. Wilkinson, eds. *Lancashire Folk-Lore: Illustrative of the Superstitious Beliefs and Practices, Local Customs, and Usages of the People of the County Palatine*. London: Frederic Warne and Co., 1867.

Herbermann, Charles G. Ph.D., LL.D., Edward A. Pace Ph.d., D.D., Conde D. Pallen Ph.D., LL.D., Thomas J. Shahan D.D., and John J. Wynne S.J., eds. *The Catholic Encyclopedia: An International Work of Reference on the Constitution, Doctrine, Discipline, and History of the Catholic Church*. Vol. 5. New York: Robert Appleton Company, 1909.

Hunter, Robert. "Astrology." In *Encyclopedic Dictionary: A New and Original Work of Reference to All the Words in the English Language*. Vol. 1 of A-Cab. London: Cassell, Petter, Galpin, and Co., 1879.

Jirsch, Anne. *Cosmic Energy: How to Harness the Invisible Power Around You to Transform Your Life*. Woodbury, Minnesota: Llewellyn Publications, 2010.

Kunz, George Fredrick. *The Curious Lore of Precious Stones*. Philadelphia: J. B. Uppincott Company, 1913.

Layard, Austen Henry. *Nineveh and Babylon: A Narrative of a Second Expedition*. London: John Murray, 1867.

Lowrie, Walter. *Monuments of the Early Church*. New York: The MacMillian Company, 1906.

Lyons, Daniel, PhD. "Stichomancy." In *The American Dictionary of the English Language*, edited by Daniel Lyons PhD. New York: Peter Fenelon Collier, 1899.

Macfarquhar, Colin, and George Gleig, eds. *Encyclopædia Britannica or A Dictionary of Arts, Sciences, and Miscellaneous Literature*. 3rd ed. Vols. I. V. Edinburgh: University of Michigan, 1797.

Mackay, Charles, LL.D. *Memoirs of Extraordinary Popular Delusions*. Vol. 1. New York: Office of the National Illustrated Library, 1852.

Murray, James A.H., ed. *A New English Dictionary on Historical Principles*. Part III ed. Batter-Boz. Oxford: Macmillan and Co., 1887.

Ogilivie, John. "Besom." In *The Imperial Dictionary of the English Language: A Complete Encyclopedic Lexicon, Literary, Scientific, and Technological*, New ed., edited by Charles Annadale. London: Blackie and Sons, 1882.

———, ed. *The International Standard Bible Encyclopædia*. Vol. 1 of *A-Clemency*. Chicago: The Howard Severance Company, 1915.

Palmer, Abram Smythe. "Poppet." In *Folk-Etymology: A Dictionary of Verbal Corruptions or Words Perverted in Form or Meaning By False Derivation or Mistaken Analogy*. London: George Bell and Sons, 1882.

———. "Talisman." In *Folk-Etymology: A Dictionary of Verbal Corruptions or Words Perverted in Form or Meaning By False Derivation or Mistaken Analogy*. London: George Bell and Sons, 1882.

Report and Transactions of the Devonshire Association for the Advancement of Science and Art. Vol. 32. 2nd ser. Plymouth: W. Brendon and Son, 1900.

Rines, George Edwin, ed. *The Encyclopedia Americana: A Library of Universal Knowledge*. V. Vol 1. New York: The Encyclopedia Americana Corporation, 1918.

Ripley, George, and Charles A. Dana, eds. *The American Cyclopædia Volume X: Kinglet – Magnet*. 10th rev ed. New York: D. Appleton and Company, 1875.

Roche Forlong, James George. *Faiths of Man: A Cyclopædia or Religions*. Vol. 3 of *Vol III - N-Z*. London: Bernard Quaritch, 1906.

Skeat, Walter William. "Anoint." In *A Concise Etymological Dictionary of the English Language*, New ed., by Walter William Skeat. Oxford: Clarendon Press, 1901.

———. "Chimes." In *A Concise Etymological Dictionary of the English Language*. Oxford: Macmillan and Co., 1882.

———. "Pendulum." In *A Concise Etymological Dictionary of the English Language*. Oxford: Macmillan and Co., 1882.

———. "Potion." In *A Concise Etymological Dictionary of the English Language*. Oxford: Macmillan and Co., 1882.

———. "Pupa." In *A Concise Etymological Dictionary of the English Language*. New York: Harper and Brothers, 1882.

———. "Rune." In *A Concise Etymological Dictionary of the English Language*. New York: Harper and Brothers, 1882.

———. "Runes." In *A Concise Etymological Dictionary of the English Language*. Oxford: Macmillan and Co., 1882.

———. *The Science of Etymology*. Oxford: Clarendon Press, 1912.

———. "Statue." In *A Concise Etymological Dictionary of the English Language*. Oxford: Macmillan and Co., 1882.

Smith, Arthur Hamilton. *A Guide to the Department of Greek and Roman Antiquities in the British Museum*. London: British Museum Department of Greek and Roman Antiquities, 1899.

Smith, Benjamin Eli, A.M., L.H.D. "Libanomancy." In *The Century Dictionary and Cyclopedia: An Encyclopedic Lexicon of the English Language*, Rev. ed., edited by William Dwight Whitney Ph.D., LL.D. Vol. 5. New York: The Century Co, 1911.

Smith, Charles John. "Talisman." In *Synonyms Discriminated: A Dictionary of Synonymous Words in the English Language*, edited by Henry Percy Smith. New York: Henry Hold and Company, 1904.

Stormonth, James. "Bibliomancy." In *Etymological Pronouncing Dictionary of The English Language*, 5th, rev. ed. Edinburgh and London: William Blackwood and Sons, 1879.

Trumbull, Henry Clay. *The Covenant of Salt: As Based on The Significance and Symbolism of Salt in Primitive Thought*. New York: Charles Scribner's Sons, 1899.

Wedgewood, Hensleigh. "Bor-Burin." *In A Dictionary of English Etymology*. Vol. 1 of A-D. London: Trübner and Co., 1859.

Wedgwood, Hensleigh. "Cauldron." *In A Dictionary of English Etymology*. Vol. 3 of A-D. London: Trübner and Co., 1859.

———. "Cord." In *A Dictionary of English Etymology*. Vol. 3 of A-D. London: Trübner and Co., 1859.

———. "Mortar." In *Dictionary of English Etymology*. Vol. 2 of E-P. London: Trübner and Co, 1862.

Whitney, William Dwight. "Amulet." In *The Century Dictionary and Cyclopedia*. Vols. Volume I. New York: The Century Co., 1906.

———, ed. *The Century Dictionary: An Encyclopedic Lexicon of the English Language*. Vol. 3 of *Volume III*. New York: Century Co., 1906.

Wilkinson, John Gardner. *A Popular Account of the Egyptians*. Rev ed. New York: Harper and Brothers, 1854.

Wilson, Harry. *Why and Wherefore? Simple Explanations of the Ornaments, Vestments, and Ritual of the Church*. Milwaukee, Wisconsin: The Young Churchman Co, 1897.

Worth, Thomas. *English Bells and Bell Lore: A Book on Bells*. Edited by William Beresford. Leek: T. Mark, 1888.

Wright, Dudley. "The Affinity of Druidism with Other Religions." *The Open Court*, January 1921, 129-141.

About the Authors

Dayna Winters

Dayna Winters is a Witch, Priestess in the Dragon Warriors of ISIS Coven, and a writer. She earned an Associate in Arts from Hudson Valley Community College, and later graduated *magna cum laude* from Sage College with a Bachelor of Arts in English. Dayna is one of the co-founders and co-directors of ISIS Paranormal Investigations in Upstate New York, and the co-host of *ISIS Paranormal Radio*. Her publications have appeared in *Threads* magazine, *Crescent* magazine, *Blood Moon Rising* magazine, and *The Journal for the Academic Study of Magic*. Her radio interviews include *Alabama ParaSpiritual* talk radio show, the *X-Zone Radio Show* with Rob McConnell, *Haunted Voices Radio*, *The Morning Rush* show on Fly 92.3 FM, and *Paranormal Radio* with Captain Jack, among others. Dayna was also featured in *Chat: It's Fate, 14 Degrees: A Paranormal Documentary*, and Discovery Channel's *A Haunting*.

Patricia Gardner

Patricia Gardner is a Witch and the High Priestess of the Dragon Warrior's of ISIS Coven in Upstate, New York. She is the co-founder and co-director of ISIS Paranormal Investigations, and she co-hosts the *ISIS Paranormal Radio* show. She has had publications appear on isisinvestigations.com, unexplained-mysteries.com, ghost-mysteries.com, and haunted-Voices.com. Her radio, television, and film appearances include *Alabama ParaSpiritual* talk radio show, the *X-Zone Radio Show* with Rob McConnell, *Haunted Voices Radio, The Morning Rush* show on Fly 92.3 FM, *The Soul Salon, Paranormal Radio* with Captain Jack, *Psychic Wisdom* with David James, *Encounters with the Paranormal*, and *The Gut and Bone* show. Patricia has also been featured in *Chat: It's Fate, 14 Degrees: A Paranormal Documentary*, and Discovery Channel's *A Haunting*.

Angela Kaufman

Angela Kaufman is a Witch, Priestess in the Dragon Warriors of ISIS Coven, and a Licensed Clinical Social Worker with over six years of experience working with individuals with mental health and substance abuse issues. She is also a professional Tarot card reader and the owner of *Moonlight Tarot*. She has had several articles published on *ISIS Paranormal Investigations;* she is a psychic artist for the latter ghost investigation group, and she has had publications appear in *Wisdom* magazine. Her radio, television, and film appearances include *The Morning Rush* show on Fly 92.3 FM, *14 Degrees: A Paranormal Documentary*, Discovery Channel's *A Haunting*, and the *ISIS Paranormal Radio* show.

Dayna, Patricia, and Angela are also the coauthors of *Wicca: What's the Real Deal? Breaking Through the Misconceptions* (Schiffer, 2011).

Index